Voices

from Within ✛

Voices
from Within ✚

Patricia Gillespie
&
Mary Mathews

A Project of the
Institute for Ecumenical and Cultural Research

Hope Publishing House
Pasadena, CA

For information address:

Hope Publishing House
P. O. Box 60008
Pasadena, California 91116 - U.S.A.
Tel: (818) 792-6123; Fax: (818) 792-2121

Scriptures quoted are from the *New Revised Standard Version Bible,* copyright © 1989 by the
Division of Christian Education of the National Council of the Churches of Christ in the
United States of America, used by permission.

Cover design - Michael McClary/The Workshop

Printed in the U.S.A. on acid-free paper.

Library of Congress Cataloging-in-Publication Data

Gillespie, Patricia.
    Voices from within : faith-life stories of women in the church /
Patricia Gillespie & Mary Mathews
       p.   cm.
    ISBN 0-932727-75-1 (pbk.) : $11.95
    1. Women in Christianity. I. Mathews, Mary. II. Title.
BV639.W7G55 1994
270.8'2'082--dc20   94-10739
                                                          CIP

in memoriam
Martha MacDonald Nelson
1927-1994

Contents ✤

Acknowledgments xi

Preface xi

Introduction xv

1 Arrival 1

2 Beginnings 13

3 The Questions and the Quest 23

4 Stories 27

5 More Stories 57

6 Worship 83

7 Meditations 91

8 Search 103

9 Your Story 123

Appendix 129

Postscript 135

Acknowledgments ✛

This book is the result of the trust and commitment of many people. While we have designed, assembled and written the actual manuscript, the ideas, advice and much of the language come from the experience and effort of others.

For financial support of the *Women and the Church Consultation* we thank Sarah P. Foxworth of Dallas, Texas, the Otto Bremer Foundation of St. Paul, Minnesota, and Theodore and Elizabeth Friend of Villanova, Pennsylvania. For providing the setting, accommodation and administration for the program we are grateful to the Board of Directors of the Institute for Ecumenical and Cultural Research in Collegeville, Minnesota, and to the institute's staff, Patrick Henry, Executive Director, and Dolores Schuh, CHM, Executive Associate.

For the work of their hearts, heads and hands, we thank the 15 women who participated with us in the four years of consultation. We are also grateful to the men who joined us at the institute for a session and the groups of women who participated in satellite sessions across the country, especially the group in Dallas who still continue to meet.

We thank Susan Carmichael who wrote the songs and those who read parts of the manuscript, helping us clarify our voices and shape our messages. For their patience and encouragement during the long months, even years, of the consultation and the book preparation, we thank our families. And for their interest in seeing some "results," which helped keep us to the task, we thank a few special friends, who know who you are.

We are grateful to you, and we hope you share our enthusiasm for the book which we all have authored, together.

—*Patricia Gillespie*
—*Mary Mathews*
Collegeville, Minnesota
The Feast of Saint Benedict

Preface ✢

Listen, my sisters—and brothers, too—and you shall hear: for we have a story to tell you. Find yourself a comfortable chair, put your feet up ... but remember, it's okay to run when the baby cries or the phone rings, because this is a story of real life, of women's lives—interruptions, tensions, distractions and all. We might have called the story "How to Find God at the Kitchen Sink."

Perhaps you were expecting theology, or a lecture on feminist spirituality. That is not our intent for we want to tell you our story, to invite you to join us on our journey. We hope you will travel with us as we each tell our own story and together explore the connections among those stories. We include here the story of our storytelling and of our growth with each other toward God.

We are "just regular" Christian women from rather diverse backgrounds interested in what the majority of Christian women in the church of North America think/feel/experience/ know about women's faith, about God, and about church, rather than what the scholars, the theologians, or even the feminists think.

At the time of our storytelling our ages ranged from 15 to 78. We are white, black, and Hispanic and come from a wide variety of denominations. Among us are teachers, students, mothers; single women, wives, widows and divorced women; a seminarian, a Benedictine sister, a former Dominican sister, a lay rector of an inner-city church, an ordained mission developer, a deprogrammed former member of a sect; an actress, a carpenter, a musician, a hospital chaplain, a consultant; a woman whose mother was a preacher, another whose daughter cannot be an acolyte; some committed feminists and some who find feminism offensive or unnecessary; women who are content with their church's roles for women and those who are unhappy with the roles their church has offered them.

We gathered to tell our stories—to listen and share the stories of women from our communities—as we prayed together, read scripture together, laughed and cried together. We listened for the patterns, the themes we share as women of the faith. No one quoted "the experts" for we agreed that we, the women—all of us, not just the 17 who met in Collegeville—are the authorities on women's faith.

As we tell our story now, we will slip from our narrative occasionally—some of us do lecture or preach on such things as theology, spirituality and women's issues and you may catch us "theologizing." But the story we tell is not forced into any systematic theology or program of spiritual development. We tell you our stories, as we hope you will tell yours, for there is truth to be found in stories and living parables that cannot be grasped by dogma or traditional theology.

Do not fear that we are treading on untested ground as we begin our spiritual journey with a story. Remember ... once upon a time, there was a rabbi, a storyteller from Nazareth ...

Introduction ✥

A young woman spoke up, "I'm going to begin here by saying that I do not have the foggiest idea where to begin."

The words she used trying to describe how she experienced a week-long gathering of women are an apt way to describe this book as well, for we would like to take you with us, as if you were present at that gathering. We met in an attempt to discover what our faith experiences mean to us and what elements may be characteristic of, or essential to, women's faith and spirituality. Despite such a defined intention, our gathering began with uncertainty and openness—quite deliberately "without the foggiest idea" of where we were headed.

Our tentative beginnings will become obvious as you peruse this meandering map of our journey. We will tell you the story of our gatherings just as they seemed to us at the time, without tidying up loose ends—which would be to fabricate, for in truth our stories, our lives, are full of loose ends and openings which allow us to travel in new and unexpected directions.

Our voices are myriad, telling our story from individual and differing perspectives, because the story is "ours," not "mine."

And so imagine us, a group of women settled comfortably in a circle, taking turns telling the story of their own experiences, building trust and confidence bit-by-bit, compiling chapter by chapter the story they lived together.

+ + + + +

In the beginning, ten of us gathered for a week-long summer meeting at the Institute for Ecumenical and Cultural Research in Collegeville, Minnesota. Our goal was to arrive at some concrete definition and articulation of women's spiritual experience, of those ways in which we know God and our church—our faith culture. Thus it happened that we began by telling one another our own stories, grounding our search in the experiences that we ourselves lived rather than in a predetermined theology we had learned.

The second summer we grew to number 17 and we struggled to list differences between our common spiritual journey as women and the male-defined one of the traditional church. Then it was we discovered many common threads weaving familiar patterns in the tapestries of our individual lives.

A Minnesota teenager commented, "Here I was, a good Catholic 18-year-old girl who had barely been past her backyard, discovering I had things in common with Presbyterians, Lutherans, Episcopalians, Disciples of Christ, Orthodox, and God-knows-what else! It just blew my mind."

A Texas grandmother from the Disciples of Christ echoed, "I did not know, nor could I imagine, that I would find my life in yours."

A Catholic homemaker added, "I have heard my heart speak with your voice, with your song, with your tears."

A Lutheran pastor from California responded, "I found myself living in the life of each of us."

The study progressed further as we considered the stories of women in the "satellite groups" of our home communities. Our list of themes blurred, becoming vague and elusive. At the same time, however, our perception grew still stronger that as Christian women we did indeed share something extremely valuable that has gone unrecognized or undervalued by the normative, traditional Christian culture.

Women's spirituality is being discussed in many places today and many are attempting to clarify, articulate or define it. We do not pretend to define for women what their faith experience is, or should be, or who they are as women and as Christians. We do want to tell you our story—the story of what happened during our gatherings in Collegeville. The pilgrimage begins with questions, uncertainty and confusion, then progresses through theories, themes and new perspectives. As the story unfolds, we invite all to share our discovery that the answers may lie in the journey itself and that our final destination is a new beginning.

Our story suggests that the gift that women's faith experience offers the church and the Christian tradition has more to do with how we approach that faith than with how we define it. What seems most significant and valuable is the process, the journey—how women live out their spiritual lives—rather than a product, a new theology to package and market.

We do not intend to define women's spirituality for them, in imitation of patriarchy. Rather our intent is to offer a framework, a model, a process which allows Christian women to discover—or perhaps, better, uncover—their spirituality for themselves in order to own and value it as part of the faith tradition.

We will rejoice if, after traveling with us, you can say as one of us did when asked to write about our gatherings: "I am afraid that this little writing project has produced more questions in my mind than answers."

We are still journeying, still questioning. The Spirit is still moving.

+ + + + +

Now, let us tell you a story: Once upon a time—actually it was July of 1985—some women traveled to Collegeville. We brought with us our faith and our fears, our understanding and our questions—and our uncertainty. Listen now as one of the younger travelers tells you of her arrival ...

1

Arrival ✤

I feel trapped. Probably I have nothing in common with anyone else here. There is another girl who showed up, but who knows? Half of me says "Don't be such a baby!" ... but the other half knows I'm not going to fit in. I am just not Ecumenical Institute material ... How did I ever end up here? I feel like laughing and crying—both.

These people don't know me. Someone else recommended I participate. They needed a young female (I hesitate to use the word "woman" because I don't think of myself as being quite that grown up).

I can't explain why I accepted the invitation. Mom thought it would be a super experience for me, and I guess for a while I believed her. By the end it took some gentle, motherly prodding (like the kind they use on cattle!) to get me out the door. I just know I am not going to like it.

Everyone is smiling. I'll bet my face looks weird. They can probably tell my smile is fake. Maybe a deep breath will help. Oh boy!

If I do stay (I wonder if I'm getting the flu—my stomach is awful), how will I ever remember all the names? Right now everybody except that other girl and the black lady—everybody else looks the same. I suppose they don't all think alike ... maybe that will help. But what if I don't understand them, what happens then? Where's Mom?

+ + + + +

The young woman takes a chair close, but not too close, to "that other girl."

A robust woman in her late thirties slips cautiously into the room and gazes toward the window. She observes ...

The room is beautiful. The wall beyond the fireplace is glass and the building sits right on the bank of a small lake. How are we supposed to work with a view like this? That looks like a great blue heron feeding on the other side of the lake.

There are name tags, notebooks, chairs and tables just like any other meeting, although the tables are arranged in a circle. There are no men. The women all look as if they know why they are here: they appear professional, prepared, ready—everything I don't think I am. Perhaps one of my kids will get sick and I can go home.

The woman who shares my apartment motions me to sit with her. We had supper together and it was a relief to know that she is as uncertain as I am. Everyone sits down and Sister Linda greets us. She doesn't look like a nun; she looks comfortable—with a warm welcoming smile and eyes that sparkle as if she might break into loving laughter in the middle of the prayer she is just beginning ...

God, our Father and our Mother, we ask your blessing on all of us who are gathered in this quiet, gentle
space. We come from different faiths, different parts of
the country with a variety of ages and occupations.

We sense, however, important elements we have in
common. We are women and we share a deep desire to
know and love you more profoundly. We have gathered
to explore the connections between these two crucial
aspects of our lives. We ask you to be with us in our
days together here. Gladden us with the sense of sisters
walking together in your light and your love ...

Sister Linda introduces Patricia. She is wearing jeans and a
man's shirt, her long hair is pulled back and there is an eager
energy in the way she presents us with a pile of papers—now
we will get down to business. I probably won't understand it,
but somehow I felt I had to come here. I guess God knows
what is going on and I guess God wants me here; there must be
some gift I am supposed to give or receive here. Lord, help me.

Patricia sits informally on the edge of the table and, after all
the usual welcoming things, continues, "At least half of you
have spoken to me already, asking me exactly what it is that we
are supposed to be doing here this week. I guess I am glad you
don't understand exactly what we are going to do and why we
are here because Linda and I don't really know either. That's
what we want to find out."

I stare at both sisters and decide: Oh great! Now I really
think I should go home.

"Before we go on to talk about the 'whys' I need to tell you
a bit about the 'hows' of the important things—where the
coffee and other amenities are. We need a little time tonight,
too, for introductions and to tell you a bit of background about
the institute and this project—basically the rules of the game."

So we discuss the setup. Patricia doesn't tell us what to do, she asks us. This is a bit uncomfortable—it would be easier if she'd just take charge, but we get used to it. We rearrange the schedule and the room. The meeting room now looks like a living room—we can sit on the sofas and prop our feet up.

Patricia introduces some institute guidelines: we are to speak in the first person, telling our own story and not hiding behind the opinions of the experts. That's not too hard for me since I don't know too much about "the experts." If I only have to know about myself, then I can't make too many mistakes, can I? Another institute tradition is that such consultations are open-ended: we are not required to produce any specific document or conclusions. Then she adds our own ground rules, which have been designed just for our group:

1). Everyone has a right to equal participation.

Patricia explains: "Just because the woman sitting next to you has her doctorate and has published six books, while you didn't finish high school, doesn't give her any more right to speak than you have. Just because the person next to you has lived a life of monastic commitment to prayer for years, while you aren't sure you agree with your church about anything, does not mean that what you have to say is less significant. We are all here as peers, equals with each other and before God."

2). Everyone has a right to pass.

"If we are uncomfortable with a question, we do not have to answer and no one should hold that against us."

3). No put downs.

4). Don't hurt others or yourself.

"Be gentle with yourself as well as others. We often tend to neglect ourselves, to care for others first."

5). Help create a safe atmosphere.

"We want to establish a sense of security and trust among ourselves. This is not just my responsibility, or Linda's, or the responsibility of which person happens to be facilitating at the time. It is a group responsibility. We are all responsible for seeing we feel safe and comfortable together here."

6). Everyone has the right to disagree.

"Each of us has a right to express her own opinion."

As I listen to the ground rules, I am wondering what dangerous operation we have undertaken so that safety is so important. Patricia tells us that the "why we are here" will be discussed after the introductions and that we need a break first. I head for the kitchen; so does everyone else. In the kitchen we are comfortable, at home. Maybe we could meet here?

+ + + + +

Polite conversation accompanies the women from the safety of the kitchen interlude back to the business of that first evening. Patricia asks the group to take several minutes now to become acquainted with those sitting nearby. In workshop terminology, the exercise is a "mixer"—the purpose is to present one another to the group ...

"I'll volunteer to begin. My name is Barbara, but I want to introduce to you Katie—who, as you can guess, is our youngest member. She is a high school student from Pennsylvania, a swimmer and a musician and a good student. She is active in her family's church and unlike some of her friends, enjoys the church services and the fellowship. She has two sisters and a happy family. Katie is unsure that she has much to offer us, but she needn't fear" ...

"I am Katie and this is Renée. We're sitting together because it feels safer! Renée is a college student, studying biology. She comes from nearby and is the fourth of five children in her family. Renée also swims, likes college a lot and thinks she's just an ordinary student with not much experience" ...

"It's all true! But sitting next to me is a lady with a lot of experience. Susan is from Texas and has three grown sons and some special grandchildren. She is patiently waiting for her first great-grandchild. Recently her husband of a lifetime died and she misses him tremendously, but is grateful for the good and full years they had together. Susan taught college when she was young and has always been active in her community and her church, the Disciples of Christ. She is very happy she was asked to come" ...

"I also think I might like rides to the cafeteria sometimes— it's a lot of walking! I want you to meet Roberta, from Minneapolis. We two have lived lots of years. Roberta was raised in the South, the only child in a very religious family. She has raised her children in the North and attempted to give them the faith which she received. Roberta does a lot of work for her black community, her church as well as the schools and social justice institutions. This lady has worked very hard and has done some wonderful things" ...

"God has been very good to me. For example, God has just let me meet Elizabeth, sitting here. Originally from Minnesota, for years she has lived in Washington. She consults, gives seminars and writes books and articles. Much of her work has to do with analyzing and directing social action organizations. She hadn't been active with her Catholic religion for years until an old friend and teacher encouraged her to try again" ...

"I feel very new in this faith business, but I will try. I can tell already that Grace, beside me here, will help me. Grace lives in Washington, too, where she writes and consults on Hispanic perspectives in the Catholic church. She was born in the Dominican Republic and spent several years in a convent, but now she dedicates her personal life and energy toward raising her young daughter" ...

"Unlike most of us, I have been to the institute before, but this is a very different beginning. I am introducing Marilyn, another Minnesotan, who now lives and works in California. After Marilyn raised a family of four, she entered divinity school. She feels fortunate to have been able to take up a new course and she is now a Lutheran minister. Her husband retired from his medical practice to go with her to start her church. Marilyn is quiet, but I think she has a lot to say" ...

"I think we all have things to say. Gail, here, surely does. She spends her energy and time in great dedication, as the lay missionary and director of an inner-city Episcopal mission in Florida. Gail knows Spanish and composes songs, which are both helpful in her work. She does leather work as a hobby. Another important thing—she has brought her guitar along" ...

"You all will have to sing with me, including my new friend, Nora. She is the mother of four and she has lived most of her life in this area. She used to teach, but now is busy at home with obligations to family and friends. She volunteers a good bit, in typical church and school and community work"...

"I have to admit I'd rather talk than sing, but I'll try. I'd like you to meet Caroline, a grad student working on a masters in divinity from Yale. The world is small—she has a professor who was my childhood neighbor. Caroline was raised in the East and has always been a serious student and has done much personal searching. She knits for relaxation and is thinking about going to seminary" ...

"When I feel stressed from work, I'll think of Dianne whom I want to introduce to you. She also is a student-type, but in addition she is a wife of a busy professor, a mother, a theater-lover, an activist and a prospective law school student. Dianne's religious background is Orthodox, which has heavily influenced her and her marriage. She seems to love life" ...

"I do love this place. My husband and I have spent time here before and I can witness to what special places this institute and the abbey are. Gabrielle, whom I am happy to introduce, shares my enthusiasm for our Benedictine hosts, although she is more familiar with the community of sisters down the road than she is with the monks here. Gabrielle is from Minnesota, has raised a family and been a "young matron" in her community. She still spends time helping her children, but she has made some changes along the way. Gabrielle is now pursuing an acting career and has a one-woman show" ...

"I seem to have taken the long way to an independence of spirit and a sense of direction, but I'd like you to meet a woman who must have been born strong. Karen was a social worker in her first career and is now a seminary teacher and social activist. She is mother to four children who are still at home—a parsonage—because her husband is a Methodist pastor. Karen was born into a ministerial family and she has lived lots of places. She and her family are now in Michigan. Incidentally, Karen's sister is an opera singer, so perhaps she can help us stay on key" ...

"I was reared on those Southern Protestant hymns, but will they sound the same up here in the shadows of a Catholic abbey? Maybe Terese, sitting next to me, can answer. She is a

Catholic chaplain in a hospital in Illinois and is married to a professor. They have two daughters and a son. Terese deals in a lot of tragedy on her job, but it's easy to see she has a lot of faith. She has always been a quiet person and comfortable with her spirituality. She reads a lot" ...

"I normally don't attend things like this, but I will try to help. My faith was shaped by the women in my family and I am comfortable talking about these things with women. Joyce, whom I introduce to you, has had a different experience. She is Orthodox and has always lived easily and faithfully within the male-directed structure of her church. Also, she has attended institute consultations before and knows where the pop and coffee are! Joyce and her husband live in the Twin Cities, where she works at the capital, keeps tabs on her grown children and gives service on church committees" ...

"Don't we all give service! The woman I introduce to you surely has. Helen has lived and worked in the area practically all her life. She comes from a big central Minnesota farm family and is a professional educator and college administrator. Her special interest is in formation of young people and this consultation subject interests her because she has done research on the different learning approaches of young women and men" ...

"I've observed some very intriguing patterns in my years of teaching, so I am really interested in our consultation subject and happy to be here. This is Barbara—born in Florida and schooled in Pennsylvania. Now Barbara lives with her family just miles from St. John's. She is primarily a mother at this stage, caring for her own family and many foster children when they need temporary homes. Barbara seems to be a permanent student and questioner, no matter what her daytime tasks are. She is competent at many things—horses and carpentry and

Girl Scouts as well as theology."

With the introductions complete, Patricia resumes discussing the project the women are about to undertake.

"The idea behind this consultation really isn't new, or 'mine.' It has just been sitting out there waiting for someone to examine it. Linda and I are happy that you all have heard whatever it was we said and that you have come tonight. No one is especially at ease now, but things will get more familiar soon, or else our whole idea is wrong. We managed to complete a circle of introductions, so we have already done something—we have drawn our first pattern and a circle is a good shape with which to begin.

"I do want to make three additional introductions, of women who are not physically here but are part of our experience. Perhaps we recognize that we have met them before ...

"The first is Anne, tall with shoulder-length, straight blonde hair and green eyes. She is 38, a divorced Catholic mother of two daughters. Born in Denmark, she was raised and educated in the U.S. and now lives in Pennsylvania. Anne practices psychology, with a special interest in battered and abused women. She is goal-directed, introspective and quiet—and writes poetry.

"The second is Sandra, a large and gentle woman of 55, with brown doe-eyes and a timid smile. She grew up as the lone sister of four brothers. Sandra expresses some anxiety about her attitudes toward God, but nevertheless professes faith in God's love. Sandra has never married, but enjoys a community of friends and a satisfying secretarial job in a Wisconsin city.

"The third is Maria, the spiritual sister of Karen whom Karen met on a trip to Central America. Maria is in her forties, but both in her demeanor and appearance she is old beyond her years. She comes from a large Catholic family and has borne eight children herself. Many of her family members have been killed or harmed during the political and military turmoil in her country. Maria is confused, mournful, beyond anger. She prays constantly for peace, but has little hope that it will come.

"Let us take these women into our circle, as we begin to explore together our experiences."

2

Beginnings ✤

The baby pours juice down the front of my dress and claps in delight. I am the only one foolish enough to have arrived with children at this social gathering of theologians and academic types. Two monks appear at my side offering their cocktail napkins, destroying my hope that no one noticed. I hand my daughter to the monk with the beard (she loves to pull beards), accept the napkins from the other and begin to clean up the mess. Retrieving my drink, I escape to the deck, knowing there is no hope of disentangling the baby from her new friend.

Yes, yes. This really was the beginning of the story—of our stories of women's experience of the church, of God. It was at this party at the institute six years before we women gathered where the questions and the ideas, which were the beginnings of this book, first surfaced. The picture of the small girl in the arms of the Benedictine monk was perhaps not out of place.

Out on the deck, there seem to be three options for social-izing—a heated debate about social justice in a small Central American country, a discussion about liturgy and preaching in Southern black churches and, of course, the Minnesota Twins. I had missed The Game and my awareness of current events was limited to close-to-home happenings (like the baby's newest tooth) but I had grown up in the South and had been the only white kid in my Bible school, so ...

An engaging black man interrupts the conversation and welcomes me with a grin (we've met before) saying, in spite of the nearly-dry-now stain decorating my dress, "You're lookin' good!" I am glad of the reassuring welcome. I had been feeling rather out of place—spending all day at home with small children isn't the best preparation for theological discussions. (Or is it?)

Waving his drink dangerously, he continues the conversation about the black church's struggle to preserve its identity—its own particular way of being Christian, of worshipping—now that black people are being accepted into white seminaries and church organizations. As I pass the cheese tray to him, he voices his concern that the black traditions, which are not part of the mainline, accepted, normative (white) church, ought to be recognized and valued, instead of being swallowed up in a kind of melting-pot ecumenism which could be fatal to minor-ity cultures.

Others in the group pick up the discussion while my mind races. There is something so familiar about what he has just said; I have felt that way myself, yet I am not black. I am so caught up in the conversation that I belatedly notice my older daughter is busily lining up the radishes and cauliflower from the relish tray all along the deck rail. Trying not to lose my train of thought, I rescue the few vegetables left on the tray and observe that this distraction is typical of women's experience—one of the many ways women seem to live in a different world, almost a different culture, within the one perceived and projected as the norm.

Eureka! That's it. The problems of the black church, of a different tradition within the larger normative one, sound familiar because I too am part of a different, non-normative tradition, perhaps a different culture, within the dominant one. Although we are the majority, women, like blacks, are marginalized—ours are not the characteristics and perspectives which are valued by the institutional church. What, then, does that mean about women and the church? About women's faith? About our traditions? About our spirituality? ... The monk is returning the baby. I don't suppose I could have expected him to know how to change the diaper.

I retreat to the bedroom with both girls; I need time alone to think anyway. I am being overwhelmed by so many new thoughts all at once, my head can hardly process them. It is an intellectual ravishment. I think that I may become pregnant.

Questions begin to blossom in my head ...

- Is my experience as a woman in the church different enough from the experience of a man that it might be a whole different culture hidden within the dominant and accepted traditions of the church?
- Do women have their own distinct set of traditions and experiences, ways of knowing and understanding our God, our faith and our church?
- Are we, like the blacks, a distinct sort of faith or church within "The Church"?

- If so, what happens to our "culture" when we are allowed full participation in the dominant one? Will we leave our women's faith, our women's spirituality, our women's theology, our "culture" as Christian women behind us before we even are aware of what it really is?
- And what is "it" anyway?
- Do we want to discover it—to own and value it equally to that of the dominant, male-defined tradition? Or do we just want to rush in and become "male Christians," accepting that what they have is more valuable?
- Is woman's faith less valuable? Is woman's way of knowing God less true?

The questions are endless and wildly exciting.

It is a long pregnancy. I struggle with these ideas like morning sickness. I try repeatedly to communicate something about women's experience of God and of the church being very different from the accepted one. The women I talk with nod and add their thoughts, their ideas, their stories to mine. Words fail us, but we feel we have something. Whatever it is, it's growing inside many of us, waiting to be born.

We strive over and over again to communicate this something to men. Many shrug, some really listen, some are intrigued, but all are baffled. One who listens is the director of the nearby Institute for Ecumenical and Cultural Research. He thought we might get some women together there to talk about it, if I could convince his board, if I could get funding ...

Instead, I get pregnant. No, not with an idea or a dream this time. I mean really pregnant. And my family is my first priority, so I do not talk with the board of the institute, I do not write grant proposals. I eat crackers, I waddle when I walk, I time contractions. I have a son, I exhaust myself with the wonder of three young, healthy children ... And ... I continue to listen to the women I meet and read the feminist theologians. I am still pregnant with this bothersome, persistent idea.

I like the feminists; mostly I agree with them; but I am suspicious. I like the women of the church too—you know the ones I mean—those of us in the kitchen, on the committees, in the choir. And many of the women of the church do not like the feminists. The feminists tell us that the men have sold us a bill of goods, defined us without asking us who we are—and now, the feminists turn around and tell us who we are.

I do not like it that a few women, though they may speak brilliantly with our women's voices, try to tell us, the women of the church, who we are and what we believe. I also suspect they do not mean to do that, but that is the way they sound and that is what many women believe "the feminists" have been trying to do.

Even though I want to know what the feminist theologians say, what I want more is to talk theology with the women on the altar guild. They would be afraid to talk "theology," but they know theology—they know God and that's what theology really is. Why a woman's way of knowing and loving God—our theology—is different from the primarily male-defined theology of the dominant culture and traditions of the Christian church is something I want to explore. I am afraid that our faith experience, our spirituality, will be abandoned by women as we are finally—and justly—offered a chance to share faith experiences and roles which have traditionally belonged exclusively to men. But women's theologizing needs to be safeguarded because what we have should not be lost. I want to treasure it and pass it on to my daughters ... and my son.

Even though I seem to have lofty aspirations, what I discover, talking with women—in church kitchens and nurseries, after committee meetings, in the seminaries and the supermarket—is that I am not alone. We, the women of the church, want to understand what it means to be female and Christian, to experience God and the church. Even those women who have insisted that women's faith experience is the same as men's, are intrigued by the question.

> *Is this now more to the point? Closer to the reason you picked up this book to begin with? Isn't all that stuff about babies and feeling uncertain in theological discussions beside the point? ... or is it? After all, this is integral to a women's life. Will we now adopt the masculine tradition of the church and compartmentalize our lives, separating our experience from our understanding of God?*
>
> *It seems that all the distractions, crying children and messy jobs play an integral part in how we approach God and the church. Our God lives not only in the solemn sanctuaries and hushed libraries of the schools of theology, but in potty training, skinned knees, hectic work schedules—in the bread and the wine.*

So, still contemplating women's experience of self, of church and of God—women's stories—and how these stories connect with our knowledge of God, some years later I return to writing grant proposals to convince the board of the Ecumenical Institute that this is something worth gathering a group of women together to talk about.

Preparing for the birth of this idea, I realize I need a midwife—someone to share the dream and as well as the travail—writing the proposal. The Ecumenical Institute has a tradition of co-facilitators for their groups, usually one Protestant and one Catholic. It should be easy for me, a Protestant living almost in the shadow of the largest community of Benedictine women in the world, to find a Catholic woman interested in such faith issues. With not a little fear and trembling, I knock on the convent door.

+ + + + +

Sister Linda continues the story ...

Patricia and I exchanged introductory greetings at the door and her question came almost before she crossed the threshold: "I need to know if you would be interested in helping with a grant application."

What an easy question to answer, I thought. This was the spring of 1985 and I was in the process of finishing my eighth and final year as academic vice-president at the College of St. Benedict. The last thing in the world I wanted to get involved in was formulating a grant proposal. My experience with that demanding task had led me to claim that to help write a grant is as arduous a task as shearing a sheep with an eyebrow tweezers.

She parried with, "Would you at least be willing to listen to the major ideas involved in the grant? The project revolves around women and spirituality." Thus my attention was hooked and a week later I found myself doing what I had been so confident I could easily avoid.

Patricia explained that for some time she had been intrigued by a phenomenon occurring in the church. While churches are beginning to share with women the decision-making processes and leadership roles that have traditionally belonged to men, her concern was that as women undertake the new roles, they may leave behind those components which have traditionally been their own. Women's faith experiences and our religious traditions—which are rarely valued by the dominant church culture—might be abandoned by the women themselves.

There were additional questions on Patricia's mind: Do women's experiences of God and the church mean something different to us than they do to men? Can these experiences be articulated and are they of value? Can they be explained to men in such a way that faith traditions which have been associated with women can be shared with the whole church as traditionally male roles in the church begin to open to women? For genuine unity and equality of the sexes within the church, shouldn't the traditions of each be valued and open to all?

An analogy occurred to me when we discussed this. In our culture we maintain a fallacy about the melting pot theory. As immigrants and other minority groups in the U.S. became amalgamated into the dominant culture, they relinquished many of their own cultural characteristics. Only now are we beginning to realize what we have lost in the homogenizing effect of the melting pot.

Christian women are not a minority group, but they have been marginalized in the male-dominated culture of the church. Will they blend in as they find their way into the center of church, giving up essential characteristics of their own culture and traditions, as our immigrants did? These were fascinating questions. What it seemed we needed was a framework to study these issues—and the funds to do so.

During the preceding decade the Institute for Ecumenical and Cultural Research had developed a program that specialized in identifying ecumenical issues that cut across traditional church boundaries. The articulation of women's faith experience regardless of denomination would seem an appropriate issue to be sponsored by the institute. This led us to a grant from the Otto Bremer Foundation which provided the funds to get started.

The participants we looked for needed to represent a diversity of denominations, age, experience, cultures, orientation toward the church (liberal and conservative) and orientation toward feminism (positive or negative).

Our hope, as we prepared for the first gathering that July, was to have women in dialogue about women's faith experiences. We knew, however, that with a group this diverse we could reasonably expect not dialogue, but major battles. The group appeared to have only three things in common: we were all Christian, all women and all articulate.

As group facilitators, Patricia and I anticipated fireworks at the mention of the priesthood for women, interpretation of Scripture, feminism, foreign policy, abortion, the president, or anything at all controversial. We began to wonder about the wisdom of such a gathering—in the end would we have anything at all to say to each other?

We sent out invitations; the women responded with astonishment and acceptance. Many couldn't believe we really wanted them to come and hear what they had to say. Some wondered if they had anything to say, but everyone planned to arrive—even if they weren't sure why. We, Patricia and Linda, arrived early, waiting (again with some fear and trembling) to welcome "The Consultants for the Pilot Project on Women and the Church at the Institute for Ecumenical and Cultural Research."

If we had enough words perhaps they would think we knew what we were doing here.

3

The Questions and the Quest ✛

The women filter back to the meeting area after the first evening's kitchen break. While Patricia readies her materials, several awkward conversations continue within the otherwise subdued gathering. A professional-looking woman in dignified skirt and jacket silently takes her seat and observes ...

This is one of the most unusual meetings I have attended and I spend a lot of my time at meetings. When are we going to set the agenda? I came to work. Issues of women's spirituality are essential for the growth of today's church and I thought our intention was to articulate what women's faith experience is. We have wasted half of this first evening chatting and rearranging furniture. Extremely inefficient. And all that time with introductions—we have our name tags and will get to know one another soon enough if this meeting is like the others I attend. A fascinating group though; I wonder if we have anything to say to each other.

Now, at last, we are getting a focus. Patricia is going to read from the grant proposal which will give us a sense of the agenda. I already made a point of asking to see the proposal. It is quite good. This is what she reads to us:

> Many churches today are considering the place of women in the church in an attempt to allow the majority to participate as "first-class citizens." We must all take care that an essential part of our faith is not lost in the changes that may result.
>
> Uniting women and men as true equals in faith and in the church is an essentially ecumenical mission and as such this union must be achieved without neglecting the traditions and experience of either party. In the effort to achieve ecumenical union and equality of the sexes in the church, women's traditions and experience—our culture—could be lost. Our proposal is an attempt to find a scheme by which this endangered culture can be articulated for ourselves, made intelligible for men and transmitted to our daughters and sons.
>
> True unity and equality requires not only that women be allowed to share the traditional male experience of faith, but also that men learn and share women's experience of faith, which has until very recently been almost completely ignored.
>
> Women's experience of God and the church has most certainly been treated as second class, but such treatment does not make the experience itself second class. God did not send Christ as a first-class citizen. Male Christians have shared Christ's sex and leadership role. Female Christians have been the suffering servants. In our striving to share the traditionally male roles in the church we must not forget or belittle our own experience as women of faith in the church.
>
> We propose to bring together at the institute a group of women for a pilot project to discover what this experience means to them and what elements are characteristic of, or essential to, women's faith and spirituality. Has our life as women, shaped by the sex-role-stereotyping traditions of our church and society, resulted in an understanding of God and ways of confessing faith and witnessing that differ significantly from those of men?

If the pilot group discovers a woman's faith experience that ought to be included in achieving an equality of the sexes in the church, we would consider how to organize a larger group into an institute consultation, the aim of which would be to explore and express our Christian experience so it can be shared with men as they are beginning to share their faith experience with us.

This project would not attempt to address directly whether a woman's theology is a result of "nature" (e.g., the experience of motherhood) or "nurture" (e.g., the effects of sexist language). The question is not "Why is our experience different?" but "What sort of faith results from the different experience?" and "How can this women's faith be communicated?" We also would not directly address traditional feminist issues such as abortion and women's priesthood, although these issues certainly affect our experience and faith.

We do not question the seriousness and timeliness of the issues that have come to the fore in the women's movement, but our proposal is focused on the articulation of women's experience rather than on the specification of imbalances and injustices. Women's experience is of course shaped by the oppressive realities of sexism, but we are not primarily concerned to identify those realities. Many individuals and groups are hard at work at that task. What we envision is a different undertaking, better suited to the size of the institute and its traditions of first-person dialogue.

Patricia continues, "Now that I have done my duty and told you what we are supposed to be doing, you can forget it. Linda and I will have it in the backs of our minds and will provide only a general focus and direction. One of the many blessings of our situation is that we are not required to have a set goal; we are free to go in whatever direction the Spirit calls us."

At last we review the tentative schedule. I bet we will spend most of our time gossiping in the kitchen. I think we are going to need more concrete aims and guidance. Now she is talking about leadership of the group " ... and we want to share the responsibility. Recalling both the right to participate and the right to pass, we are asking that everyone share the leadership and the recording duties."

They have made up lists of meeting sessions, worship times, secretarial duties and we are supposed to sign up. Do these women have any idea how much work they are making for themselves later? It is easier for one person to do it all. Well, I will sign up to help. If nothing else, we may have an interesting study in the workability of this "feminist circular style leadership." It looks more like total chaos than leadership.

Sister Linda is about to close the session with prayer. I hope some people stay around to talk—that woman just back from Ethiopia or the one with the inner city church, or ...

4

Stories ✛

Miles and miles and miles and miles
We will walk just to touch but the hem of your garment.
Oh miles and miles, for, Lord, when we touch you,
It's then we are truly made whole.

Miles and miles we'll walk through all emptiness,
Miles and miles through desert and wilderness,
Miles and miles through sin and self-centeredness,
We'll touch you and we'll be whole.

Miles, the miles you walk with us patiently,
Miles and miles you time all so perfectly,
Miles and miles you do nothing hastily,
Wooing the depths of our souls.

Oh, to love you gracious and gloriously,
Oh, to love you is perfect liberty,
Oh Jesus, may our whole hearts always turn to thee,
May we be thine as we go.

Oh, to serve you faithfully, willingly
Oh, to tell the world of you joyfully,
Oh, Jesus, thank you for setting the captives free,
Our hearts sing praises, my Lord.

Miles and miles—it is a journey we have all made in our own unique stories. It is with our own stories, our own journeys that our group began our exploration of women's faith, of the ways in which we have experienced God and God's church. We can offer to you here only small pieces of each woman's path, although in our actual gathering we attempted to trace more fully our spiritual journeys and our experiences as women and as Christians.

Each woman, from either our gathering at the Ecumenical Institute or one of the "satellite" gatherings modeled on it, will tell you a part of her journey, a part which was selected because in retrospect we discovered that it was a theme or experience common to or typical of many of our stories. We also offer here a few "echoes" of each woman's story, just as in our original gathering we reflected as a group on each other's journeys.

Join us now as we gather casually and comfortably for our storytelling. There is an empty seat for you there on the sofa beside Joyce or join me here on the floor. Listen carefully and learn to know each of us, our struggles, our joy, our anger, our confusion ... our God. Listen carefully too for echoes of your own story.

Katie, eyes bright with the curiosity and uncertainty of youth, leans forward, about to speak ...

Katie

I don't know where to begin, but one of us has to start. Maybe it is easier for me because I am the "baby" of the group, so my story will be brief.

I'll start with my family. Maybe that is what is most important about who I am. You asked us to talk about who we are as women and as Christians. My search for who I am is only starting and so my journey starts with my parents and my sisters. I think that is where my faith begins, too. My family is loving and close. Somehow there are some things that I just know are true because that's the way it has always been for me.

I hear some women talking about men in negative ways and about not liking to call God "Father." That just doesn't fit my experience—although my mother is the one at home with us most of the time. My dad is a doctor and is gone a lot, but he is a gentle, kind and loving parent, too. I don't call God "Father." I call God "God."

I have led a very sheltered life—nothing sensational, no conversions or major religious experiences. So far my life has been blessedly boring in this light. My faith seems just a natural and important part of my life.

I came here reasonably sure of my faith and reasonably sure of what I, Katie Ruhland, believed. As I talk with you here, my faith in God is becoming stronger than ever. However, I am now completely confused and unable to define *what* I believe— all I know is that I believe it. There is so much I don't know about God and the church, I only know I am learning. The only things I guess I really know for sure are that there is a God, that he has a wonderful son named Jesus and that there is life after death. Maybe that's all that a sheltered 15-year-old needs to know.

O God, you are my God, I seek you ... (Ps 63:1).

The search for how we can become "most truly ourselves"
is continually intertwined in our stories with our search for

God. In many of our tales, particularly of childhood, there was an unself-conscious, natural awareness of God that underlies this search or journey.

Sandra: What you, Katie, our sheltered 15-year-old, know about God is such a gift. What we know as children is so real; sometimes it gets lost later. I remember as a small girl being out alone gathering wildflowers when suddenly I knew that God was there—really right there with me.

Karen: I'm in the middle of "mid-life crisis" and I am still searching for who I am ... or for those wildflowers and God.

Susan: Katie, I could be your grandmother and I am still searching for who I am, for what God wants of me. Our desire seems to be to become a useful, effective part of God's world, to find our "calling" and to fulfill God's purpose ... somehow there seems to be a continuous searching so we find it difficult to know when we have arrived.

Anne: Perhaps the arrival is only another beginning.

With that comment, Roberta nods in agreement, gestures invitingly with her graceful dancer's hands and begins ...

Roberta

Recently a young artist invited my daughter and me to see a film on the butterfly so my daughter could choreograph it. The butterfly emerges and travels thousands of miles under adverse conditions and survives until it's time to terminate this particular journey. Somehow the butterfly would escape its predators—a delicate butterfly in the air over the mountains—just flying.

If God takes care of this fragile butterfly, how would God take care of us? I contemplated my life and this butterfly—the miracle of the monarch butterfly and how it compares with the miracle of Roberta Lange.

Like Katie, it was my parents' preparation which enabled me to be a living miracle. All of us are miracles. When we realize that we are, our lives take on a new dimension. No matter how young or how old we are, we have some special abilities.

I'll be 69; I have now ten children and 19 grandchildren. As a child, I lived with a religious grandmother and knew the Lord's Prayer before I was four. I think she was a Baptist; we had to sit on hard seats. I was being molded and groomed.

I've been a taxi driver, a maid, a professional dancer and taught school. When my son was 30, I got an MA in public administration and ended up a housing specialist. I have had more jobs than anyone can count and at each place I got a special benefit. God wanted me to be there to prepare for the next chapter in my life. It is the grace of God that we're here.

Four years ago I developed cancer, two years ago I had a heart attack, but here I am, a walking miracle. I still teach dance once in a while just to blow people's minds that at 68 I can still do that. And I'm diabetic, but I don't worry about that. God will take care of me. He has his own time. Meanwhile, you just serve God and you just soar, you fly.

I bore you on eagles' wings and brought you to myself
(Ex 19:4).

Roberta's story is one of much adversity and oppression and yet throughout she soars. Again and again we found in our stories an acceptance (though not necessarily passive!) of unexpected, surprising and often difficult events as somehow being part of God's plan for our journey. As Roberta said, "God wanted me to be there" even when we don't understand why and even when it hurts.

Helen: Behind the happiness, Roberta, there must be a lot of pain—for example, your children have just been victims of racially-related police brutality. Also you talk about raising your children, but don't mention that your husband died close to the time the last one was born.

Roberta: I have lived all my life with restrictions, discriminations and adversities; black people and women do that. I see it and I work for justice as God makes me able. Sometimes the adversity seems to interfere or interrupt our phases of growth or service. Yet, those same experiences somehow elevate us to a higher plane as Christians—an advancing in wisdom, courage, determination and greater love.

Across the circle Susan's kind blue eyes mirror Roberta's rich dark ones and with a shared easy smile, again reflecting a long life of both smiles and tears, Susan begins her story, a gentle Southern rhythm to her voice ...

Susan

I believe my story follows Roberta's. Besides being from the same generation—and in spite of very different situations in life—I have suffered grief but not the same adversity and oppression. Since we have a lot of experiences in common, we tend to speak the same language—for example, the word "black" still comes awkwardly for me, although I have shared my life with a black woman for years. She was with me through the difficult time when my husband was dying and we have agreed to care for each other as we grow older together.

My relationship with God is very personal—a personal request for strength. I needed that strength through my husband's long illness, preparing with him for his death and now without him. My faith has always been that way, an intimate and special source of strength. In trying to understand where I got that feeling for God, I come back to the fact that I was brought up with loving discipline. My relationship with God was nurtured by my family. My parents were pillars of the church and maybe I absorbed that personal sense of God in some way from the people I knew in the church.

Sometimes I think that my religion is too private—a direct connection with God. I had trouble saying, "I pray through Jesus Christ"—that seems a detour. Go right to the top. A good lesson for life—go to the boss.

My story as a woman is very traditional. When I got married I didn't even consider continuing teaching. I was to become a helpmate, wife and mother and that is what I did. My mother and her mother had done that, and that would be fulfilling. My sense of myself as Christian and as woman connects with tradition and with my own mother.

My mother used to worry about so much; she felt her faith was not strong enough. She wanted me to be perfect. When I said to her, "I can't be perfect!" her response was, "Just try harder." She never gave me any leeway. She was a wonderful woman and she never let me go. I think I fulfilled her all right. I still struggle with perfection—spiritually and personally.

For myself, I do not say that to my children. My boys were all baptized in the Christian church for me. One said, "I'm not good enough." I said, "You're just joining a group of people who are trying to be good."

I am now at a stage where I can serve somewhere. I am still seeking that "calling" as part of the church—that group of people who are trying to be good. I am still wanting to be perfect for God. Perhaps being here will help me find a way to serve God and the church. I have my health, wonderful friends, my home. I know I must do something.

> *Be perfect, therefore, as your heavenly Father is perfect*
> (Mt 5:48).

> *The struggle for perfection in Susan's story surfaced with
> many others. Sometimes it comes from the often oppressive
> desire to please those who love us, to meet their expectations
> —realistic or not. With others it is the struggle for ongoing
> spiritual growth—the verse from Matthew after all is not in
> the context of meeting others' expectations but of learning to
> love one's enemies. Many women also echoed Susan's sense
> that one's relationship with God is deeply personal and
> intimate.*

Barbara: What society expects has been defined by males.
Perhaps we are striving for a perfection that doesn't fit us.

Elizabeth: I don't need to be perfect from society's perspective, but I want to be the most perfect expression of the precious essence of Me that God designed just for me. I want to fulfill the promise that God infused in me at my conception.

Anne: God, who knows the secrets of my heart, knows that I am so far from God's dreams for me; but it is just that intimate, personal relationship you speak of that keeps me longing to become more perfect, to fulfill those dreams.

Gail: My relationship with the Lord is so private that I have difficulty speaking of it—almost as if one of you were to invite me into your bedroom to observe your relationship with your husband.

Susan: Yes, it is that kind of special, trusted relationship with God that gave me the strength to keep going through my husband's extended illness and death.

Susan talks a bit about her long and loving marriage and

about her grief during her husband's illness and at his death. Her voice begins to shake and she ends the story mid-sentence. Terese sitting next to her on the couch turns and gently puts her hand on Susan's shoulder.

We are silent. Some of us are crying. No words are needed for us all to hear and share Terese's prayer for Susan, for the healing of her grief, the thanksgiving for her marriage and for her strength. When the time is accomplished, Terese turns back to the group and begins her story, her voice as calm and soothing as her touch ...

Terese

When I was a little girl I was very serious about my faith. I dislike talking about myself but when I think about the story of my life I always find myself returning to being a little girl. The child in me is still a treasured part of who I am today.

I took religion very seriously. For example, I wouldn't bend my knees during Mass and I used to try saying the Lord's Prayer without any other interrupting thoughts. At my first communion I felt very special, close to God. I was something of an outcast at school—too quiet and pious—sort of an outsider. Part of that may be because we moved eleven times in thirteen years.

To me women were the church because in my family only women went to church. I remember watching my grandmother reading her prayer book. As a little girl, I loved being with women, practically worshipped them. My great-grandmother who was 93 seemed a saint to me. I also thought that heaven was all women.

Even though I can appreciate many of you who, like Roberta, do so much, still I find I need a lot of time alone, for myself, for God. Although I can rejoice in the busy lives of others, I have no desire to be an overachiever. I still feel a bit of an outsider to the church. My chaplaincy is my community. In the past year I have lived with grief—I sat with a mother whose daughter died, I baptized a one-pound baby, I watched as a family sang hymns to their dying mother the last week of her life.

Yet women still shape my life—Mechtild of Magdeburg (I even gave my daughter that as her middle name), Hildegard of Bingen and other medieval women mystics. Something about the mystics fits and I have a sense of being connected with them. For the child that I was, the child that I am, the child that I hope to be, women seem to have provided for me the comfort, the healing waters, the home where my spiritual life was nourished.

"Truly I tell you, unless you change and become like children, you will never enter the kingdom of heaven" (Mt 18:3).

The little girl was a cherished part of each of our stories —not as a step to be left behind in our spiritual growth, but as a true, intimate and continuing part of who each of us is in relationship with God. Nearly every story echoed Terese's sense that the women around us, although not often vested with spiritual authority, were influential and often formative.

Gail: Perhaps children see God more clearly. Although my parents were not religious, I was aware of God at an early age. When I was seven my sister was in a jeep accident and I looked up to heaven and asked God to save her. He did.

Joyce: As a child, my life revolved around the church.

Church work, women and prayer belonged together.

Dianne: Yes, growing up in the Orthodox tradition as you and I did, meant home rituals were important—special icons, candles, incense, fasts—always the woman did that. Although we have learned about dogma from men, many of us here seem to feel that we have learned about spirituality from women.

Helen suggests that we might take a short break for coffee, drinks and snacks and we adjourn to the kitchen. Over coffee and continued discussion of Terese's recurrent little girl, Anne comments enigmatically, "Since adolescence follows childhood, perhaps it is my turn next." When we return Anne sits with her knees drawn up and her arms wrapped around her legs. We tease her about imitating the adolescent she has predicted. Tilting her head a bit to one side, she sounds a bit bemused as she begins ...

Anne

I am 38 years old and I have spent the last year as if I were again 16. This is my third adolescence—it seems to come back to me repeatedly. Things that made sense to me and were "settled" again became open to challenge. I question authority, even that same authority others look to me to find. I find myself open to hopes and dreams and fears which I thought were left behind, "outgrown." I live through emotional heights and depths of love and faith, for which my hormones cannot be held accountable as they might be at 16. I question God the same way I did when I was in high school, but God knows—and I know—the questions are different, deeper and more dangerous now—although the words I use are the same.

Sometimes I wonder if I am only trying to stay one step ahead of my daughters as they approach adolescence or if I am trying to avoid overtaking my mother and approaching death. I don't know. It's as if my life refuses to follow those neat, linear developmental patterns and keeps returning and repeating itself. Yet it is not repetition. Each return—like Terese returning to the little girl within—is not just circling back to the same place, not a spiritual journey retracing the same steps. Each time the return is deeper and stronger—more like spiraling into the depths of the earth or into the heart of God.

Every time I think I have found some stability, some maturity, and have things in place (I felt that way six years ago—my job, my marriage and my family seemed full, complete and settled and I even thought I understood something about God)—then WHAM! surprise comes. I am an infant again —suddenly vulnerable, uncertain and radically dependent on I-don't-know-what. I begin again to discover, with the astonished eyes of a child, a God of surprises. So I question, I search. I have somehow never doubted that God loves me, but I have doubted everything else. When Katie speaks of knowing how little she knows, I know that in some ways she is blessed with more certainty than I and I look to her for mothering although in years she might be my daughter.

What am I to do when I live my life in cycles and circles and I grow toward God in spirals instead of climbing ladders when the only words I have been given to explain myself, both psychologically and spiritually, are those of linear development? St. Paul speaks of leaving childish things behind when he becomes a man. For me it is in finding those childlike things anew that I find God. There are no words to explain how in being 16 for the third time my same questions probe more deeply into my own heart and into the heart of God.

Round and round goes the wind, and on its circuits the wind returns (Eccl 1:6).
The wind blows where it chooses ... (Jn 3:8).

The movement of the wind, the spirit in our lives—occasionally of hurricane force—was often seen in circular or spiral patterns in our stories. Like Anne, we often returned to the same place, yet at a newer, deeper level.

Barbara: With the birth of each of my children I circle back to the same place. The same and yet entirely new.

Gabrielle: Our female bodies keep us in cycles. Women's whole lives show this—cycles and rhythms, not goals.

Karen: Our experience—in our journeys and in our time here—suggests circular patterns rather than hierarchical ones.

Elizabeth: Perhaps there is a perspective from which we are always in transition or on a rhythmic cycle whether we acknowledge it or not.

Marilyn: Women's stories seem to demonstrate an ability to "flow"—so if their life's dreams and goals and efforts were blocked one way, they found another way to go.

Sandra: The movement is not straight and linear, but curving back on itself like a stream. I take my past, both painful and healthy, with me and try to grow on it.

The rhythmic discussion continues to flow as we break the meeting for the afternoon. Some of us explore the pottery at the monastery, others visit the craft shop at the convent. We find treasures to take home and ideas as we talk and laugh and tell stories of those at home to whom we will bring gifts.

We gather at the abbey church for a tour. In the basement closets Elizabeth extends her flair for dressing in bold and brilliant colors by modeling the priest's festive vestments. He is amused; Elizabeth is radiant in clothing that suits her well but which her church will not allow her to use. When we return to the meeting room, I still imagine her in priestly Pentecostal silk as she puts aside her equally colorful needlework, freeing her hands for the gestures that accompany her story ...

Elizabeth

I am used to directing groups, but not in talking about myself. The words I use for myself don't seem to fit into group meetings. I have worked for 22 years in responsible positions and am now on a self-styled sabbatical. I want to take the time consciously to search into my spirituality and make this congruent with my leadership in social action and education in a global way. I am very passionate about what I do and how I feel. I am trying to be open to risk, not to be too careful of myself. I feel things strongly—up or down. I have only recently come back to God and I am searching.

I don't belong to a church, but I've been "slinking around" the edges. I find words help and can talk to God easily. I'm comfortable with the word "Spirit" but have trouble with the words around Jesus Christ and Christianity. Like Anne, I have difficulty using the church's traditional words to express my spirituality. Symbols and metaphors seem to be a more natural way for me to hear, to understand and to speak. Also, I find poetry, dreams and miracles to be a comfortable vehicle for the Spirit. In talking with the women here in this safe female haven this language has been acknowledged and nurtured. I like how women talk and I did not know it.

In reading Hildegard of Bingen and Matthew Fox I find so much that fits with what I am, but not with what I thought the church was. I feel like a mystic and that I can know God through creativity and nature. I feel like I'm on a spiritual quest and I don't want to withdraw again, but I'm resistant to needing to belong to a church. Maybe I can be God's minister without belonging to a church.

I grew up in the Catholic church but later when I turned to it, it turned from me. I went to a priest when I got my divorce and he said, "Had you come to me as a person, I would tell you to get a divorce. As a priest, I have to tell you that you have to act as if you were married to this man the rest of your life. You can sleep with anyone you want if you go to confession, but if you marry again, you'll be excommunicated."

So I find my spirituality through nature: I sit and write in my journal near the redwoods and the ocean. And I continue to slink around the edges of churches, but I do not join. I don't need a place to be social, but one to be spiritual and one that accepts me and acknowledges my faith.

Sometimes you know you're special, but you don't know what to do with it.

Ah, Lord God! Truly I do not know how to speak (Jer 1:6).

Elizabeth and Anne were not the only ones among us who felt we had things to say for which we did not have the words. We debated about whether our struggle to express ourselves was the result of a male-developed language faced with peculiarly female concepts or whether we were simply trying to express essentially inexpressible spiritual experiences. In either case, many of us felt parts of our experience were best expressed in metaphor, poetry or song.

Our relationship, or non-relationship, with the church wove its way in and out of each story, resonating between centrality and marginality.

Marilyn: Many women are spiritual without being in the church. Sometimes I wonder why I'm in the church when all the spiritual people are out.

Barbara: I can imagine being spiritual without the church, but I can't be a Christian alone. For me, community is essential to Christianity.

Renée: I find community here in this group, but not always in the church. I can relate to those who feel marginal in the church.

Helen: Perhaps some of that marginalization is because we don't speak the language.

Terese: I agree with what Katie said, "Girls accept you better." I feel the language I speak is understood more by women—including my spiritual language.

Anne: Is the communication better because of a shared language or because of a communal bonding among women?

Terese: Fortunately *and* unfortunately for us the very finest goings on of the heart and soul cannot be communicated with words. The looks in your eyes have given me courage that I have not found elsewhere in *any* male or in the church.

There is a pause as we recognize together those inexpressible goings on of the heart. Karen offers them for us all in prayer:

> Jesus, our brother, in your wisdom you hear and understand the unformed words of our hearts and souls. You spoke your Good News to us in parables. Help us now to speak our own stories in words that will be heard and open our ears to listen to one another. AMEN.

Elizabeth picks up her needlework again and turns to smile encouragingly at Renée who is sitting beside her. She grins back, swings her legs over the arm of her chair and begins her story, speaking easily almost as if she were talking with her peers in a college dorm ...

Renée

When everyone first started talking, I thought I would have so much to tell. Yet I have lived a very sheltered life.

In eighth grade my family went through family therapy as one of my sisters was anorexic. I thought just the word sounded scary. Later she became an alcoholic and our family went back to therapy. During therapy my sister read a letter saying how much she hated us—our whole family was shocked. I resented her for that because I felt we were trying to support her. I was afraid of becoming like her. I kind of withdrew. I have this overwhelming fear of trying things—a fear of failure.

This year I really came into my own. With another girl I started a Christian Life committee at school and spiritually that became a big part of my life. I still have this fear when something unexpected comes up in school. I overloaded myself with classes so I wouldn't have to assess my life. Right now, just having graduated, I have a fear of the future—so many things can happen. I like things just so.

When going through this with my sister, I thought, "Why us, God?" I got angry. I do pray to God, but I haven't quite figured out where God is in my life. I'm not real church oriented. I'm a good Catholic girl. A lot that is said in church goes over my head. As a child, it didn't mean much.

I identify myself more with relationships than with ideas. That is part of why my relationship with my sister is scary— how much is she part of who I am? And with the church too— even when the ideas go over my head, I am still part of the community, of the people. A community, as I see it, implies each member has a definite sense of belonging. And here with you I feel like I belong. I feel secure and at home—it's like having a second family. It seems as if when you tell your stories I form some kind of supernatural bond with each of you as I am drawn into each of your lives. I kind of lost myself in your experiences and your emotions and it really shook me up.

"Am I my brother's keeper?" (Gen 4:9).

> *Like Renée, many of us identified ourselves through our relationships. We are more likely to define ourselves, as Roberta did, with "I am a child of God" than to say "I am a Christian." And those relationships that define and shape us are often described as family.*

Karen: We have a good biblical precedent for speaking so often, as you have done, about community as family: Jesus said that whoever does the will of his Father in heaven is his brother and sister and mother. The church should be family.

Sandra: But it is much more painful when someone in your family—someone with whom you identify—hurts you. Like Renée, it makes me frightened and uncertain about who I am.

Anne: That is when the church, or other "second families" like this, help. I am the daughter of an alcoholic. This is a painful part of my identity, but now I am also the sister of Roberta whose miraculous flight over her troubles gives me courage and hope. Each of your stories becomes a part of who I am.

And the stories continue, moving easily around the circle as Joyce hands her pen and paper to Caroline and exchanges her role as note taker for that of storyteller.

Joyce

I don't know why I am here. It must be an act of God that I am here. God puts us in certain places at certain times.

As a child my life revolved around the church. The Orthodox faith and traditions are an important part of our home life.

Prayer is an important and powerful part of my life. My son had a water skiing accident and broke both legs and his pelvis and was in a coma for weeks and I know that it is because of the power of prayer that he is alive today. Everyone was praying for him. We can do nothing without God's help.

When growing up I never felt oppressed by male authority either in church or at home, but my daughter questions it. As a young mother I did have feelings of inferiority—thinking that the things I said and did weren't important.

In the Orthodox church, which is very male oriented, I can say without any hesitation that women will never be priests. But I am comfortable with that because women do have important roles in the church. In our church men and women are equal—the only thing that women cannot do is perform the sacraments. Women are concerned with humanitarian things like sending food to the hungry, or helping orphans from the Middle East. They show by their acts what they are.

Pray without ceasing (1 Thess 5:17).

We talked a lot about prayer, about verbal prayer, about prayer with "sighs too deep for words" (Rom 8:26), about contemplative prayer and about our tendency to offer our actions to God as prayers—those women's "humanitarian things" Joyce mentioned.

And again and again our stories spoke of limits, women's limits, in our lives, in our churches.

Dianne: You do not feel oppressed by the limits the church sets on women's roles. And you accept that our Orthodox daughters cannot be priests. But I wonder if they can accept it without feeling the oppression.

Anne: Like the "good Catholic girl" who in response to her bishop's question about the number of sacraments responded, "Six for women. Seven for men." Ordination is for men only.

Katie: Or my friend who got her Bible in fourth grade and went through changing every "he" to "she."

Caroline: I experience those limits in seminary. I realize I need to become masculine to become the norm of a pastor. I need confidence in my own way of leading.

Joyce: Maybe it is because Orthodox women are so active in leading our home ritual that we don't feel oppressed. Or maybe because our time is so full of church work and prayer.

Sandra: Your service is prayer. You pray with your hands. Is women's prayer life different from men's?

Barbara: Much of my prayer is wordless. I open myself and listen.

Karen: It is little things directed toward God. Like yesterday, Barbara and I were walking back from lunch together and at the very same moment we sighed and then laughed at our togetherness. We didn't need to explain that it was a sigh of thanksgiving for all that is happening here. It was a prayer.

Susan: Prayer is that whole personal relationship with God—our actions, our words, our silence.

Barbara suggests a break or perhaps an active prayer. Joyce teaches us folk dances—a prayer of our bodies, of communal celebration. Not only are we told to "pray constantly" but also to "rejoice always" (1 Thess 5:16).

Finally we retreat to the kitchen for refreshment—and a

continuing discussion of "limits"—before we gather again in our circle, turning to face Marilyn who seems ready to share her story ...

Marilyn

I too have bashed my head up against those limits, especially the ones connected with men and the church. In seminary when I first discovered what the church system does to women I was totally shattered. I remember reading things that the church fathers said about women and bursting into tears. There have been so many men who have been important in my life which perhaps explains why my own anger has been so intense.

Although several generations of my family have grown up in America, my family still thinks of themselves as Scottish and takes pride in that. There was a strong sense of family and the head of the clan, my father, who also preached in the Presbyterian church, was a real patriarch. He ruled, but with a sense of real responsibility about it and I felt very loved and cared for. As a child I did not feel it as oppressive, only much later did I begin to see the sense of power.

My father made definite distinctions between men and women. I was like my dad, but supposed to be like my mom. As a child, I'd hide to avoid the housework, but played football. And I was ashamed of my body—it seemed so skinny and awkward that I never thought I would become a woman.

I hero-worshiped a lot and was constantly in love. Three men who were close to me died in war and my college boyfriend was killed in a car accident. I had decided there was no God—which was quite a switch—yet I remember praying, "God, I don't know who you are or even if you are there ... but if you are, help me." Gradually I realized I was talking about and talking to God.

Later, a priest said to me, "Marilyn, God loves you. Don't you think it's time you learned to love God?" That was the start of a journey that has never ended.

I have struggled with and found painful the emphasis on a male God. There was a time when my solution was to "equalize" God with a female god. But that does not work for me. In the effort, we only succeed in creating a new god in our own image and any image is limited.

All of this leaves me in a dilemma. Is it possible to be intimately associated with a God that has been stripped of all personality for the sake of awesomeness? Even in the midst of wanting to know God as the "Holy One," the God of Moses, I find myself needing a God who embraces me and is not afraid to be contaminated by my own earthiness.

I suspect that I am on a life-long journey of wondering about the nature of God.

"I AM WHO I AM" (Ex 3:14).

The nature of God and particularly the names and images which we have been given for God and which we want to use for God were frequent formal and informal topics of discussion. Although not part of our intended task, considering how God has been presented to us and how we ourselves image God came up again and again as we told our stories. Having God presented in primarily male images, as "more like them (men) than like me," cannot help but affect our experience. For some of us the struggle was more difficult, even agonizing, others seemed able to accept it with ease, but none of us could ignore it. Often the struggle was bound up with our sense of our "earthiness," of ourselves as whole people—body and spirit.

Barbara: I have no trouble imaging God as female. My experience of God is of the sort of unconditional love usually associated with mothering.

Helen: As a child, I often imagined myself sleeping in God's arms, a very maternal image. I have returned to that "resting in God" now in contemplative prayer.

Katie: But fathering can include that kind of loving also.

Barbara: Yes. I do not want to give up my image of Father-God either. I want both images, not some absolutely transcendent intangible. God is beyond images, but my experience is tangible—that She holds me and He supports me. My God is incarnate, a Real Presence.

Gabrielle: The body-soul dualism in the church seems to leave us out. We are told our bodies, especially our female bodies, are not good.

Dianne: I never felt comfortable with my body until I had my first baby. At least that baby thought I was perfect.

Barbara: Giving birth was for me a spiritual experience. That sense of new life and of unconditional love revealed a whole new dimension to my relationship with God.

Grace: It is sacramental—something physical and tangible bringing God's grace to us. It is all around us, in the holy water of baptism, in holy water of birth, in the holy water of our tears. That is sacrament. Our tears have flowed abundantly here. We could probably have washed ourselves in them and been reborn. It is in these tangible events and people that we know God.

As we look around at each other, we recall the tears. In front of the watery background, Gail begins to sing a song of rivers and grace. At the end of the song, Sandra shifts in her chair and with the holy water of tears still on her cheeks, she begins, her voice at first small and shaky, gathering strength as she speaks ...

Sandra

In my story men and God are all mixed up together. Marilyn is concerned about images for God—well, mine are still really confused.

When I was a little girl, I knew that God loved me and protected me *and* that God wore a dark suit, a navy-blue, striped tie and shiny black shoes. When I said the Lord's Prayer "our Father" looked a lot like "my father." And my father, although I did sense that he loved me, was in many ways very distant from me. When we went to church it was the men who talked, stood up front and—so I thought—who acted like God.

I have four older brothers and I was the only girl. I was treated as different, as special—dressed up in fancy clothes and protected, cherished. I tried to be what they wanted, quiet and sweet. I didn't get dirty like my brothers.

My uncle was a preacher—he had those shiny black shoes, too—and when I was little he was especially nice to me. But later when I was nine or ten I became afraid, I didn't understand why and I tried to stay away from him. But we were a close family—he lived with us most of the time—so that was difficult. It was not until I was 14 that I could admit even to myself that I was being sexually abused and that my family was ignoring it. Just seven years ago, some 40 years later—and three years after my uncle died—did God give me the courage to seek help and go into therapy.

So somehow I lost God when I was a teenager. Like Renée, I asked, "Why me, God" and did not hear any answer. God was ignoring or couldn't see my pain and confusion—just like my family had. So I guess I ran away from God, too. And still today, it hurts and I feel betrayed and abandoned if I think of God as male. (And I still run from shiny black shoes.)

I found God again because one day in my incest victim's support group, a nun who had also been an incest victim, said to me, "Can't you see, Sandy, how much God loves you? How every moment She is reaching out to hold you?"

"She?" I thought. It was like I was all ready to spit out something nasty and bitter and someone had put honey on my spoon. I burst into tears right there in front of everyone and Sister Mary Clare held me and rocked me.

It hasn't been that simple. I still struggle with who God is in my life and with how I feel betrayed by men, by my family and sometimes by God. But I do know again now, as I did when I was a little girl, that God loves me.

O taste and see that the Lord is good (Ps 34:8).

Many of our stories were of brokenness and healing. Few were as painful as Sandra's, but many were, as Katie pointed out, "frankly traumatic." The movement between brokenness and healing, the place of God and the church in that healing and the cycle of alienation and reconciliation were frequent topics of discussion and prayer.

In the silence and tears following Sandra's story, Roberta walks across the room and takes her in her arms. After a moment she says, "Child, you have been through a trial by fire and that trial has resulted in a jewel. You suffer hardships and survive the challenges and come out more beautiful."

Later we discuss stories of Biblical women. Stories, like Sandra's of pain and healing: the woman who touched the hem of Jesus' garment, the woman who begged for "the crumbs under the table" that her daughter might be healed and others. These women's stories join our stories. Before we continue with our stories, Gail and Helen have planned a ritual of healing and reconciliation ... for Sandra, for one of us who was raped, one who was assaulted, one who was threatened with rape, for all of us who have felt helpless, betrayed and broken and long for reconciliation. There is prayer, there is touching, there is song, there is healing. God is with us.

We talk quietly about forgiveness and reconciliation before our stories begin again. Gail is sitting on the floor leaning against Barbara's knees. She has put her guitar aside, paused briefly in silence and now begins her story ...

Gail

My story is much the same as everyone else's. Only the details are different. I was born into a military family, with all that means. My college major was Spanish and it turned out to be very helpful. I love to work with my hands and to trek the backwoods and hills. My trusty guitar goes with me and I sing and compose as I go.

For a while I taught high school, but I felt the Lord nudging me to move on to other tasks. Now I am an urban missionary. I've not married and while that kind of relationship would be nice, I do feel fulfilled in the Lord and I trust God's plans for my life. I have not had great personal tragedy, only the everyday hurts and longings that make life. I remember clearly when my sister was seriously injured in an accident in our childhood. It was the first time I recall really encountering God. Now I see so much tragedy around me, so much pain that needs healing and for me there is healing and understanding in trying to ease that pain. There is anguish where I am.

I am lay vicar of an inner-city mission church. I guess you could say that I am everything but the priest. The people I work with are beautiful and needy. Their hearts are looking for Christ. I see my work as helping others find wholeness in God. Some days are very long and I live a little way away from the mission, so that I can have time to refresh. The traditional church, with its structure and way of doing things, has often saddened me. But this effort of my church is so needed and so good. Here the people come to get something and we try to give them the fruits of faith—love, joy, peace, longsuffering, gentleness, goodness, meekness, temperance.

Don't misunderstand me—it is hard-fought success when it does come and our place is full of disappointments. Many of our mission folks are mentally ill, destitute, never seeing love, or never having known love. The people of the diocese trust us with the task—people who are by comparison clothed in the garments of the world. But they pay for our mission. They work through us.

I have little to say about the issue of women and men in the church—either I have ignored, been unaware of or somehow spared the oppressiveness of a, perhaps, male-oriented church. Part of our journey in Christ is, it seems, deliverance from the oppressive extremes of either the pharaoh or the Jezebel. What I want to change is hearts. Only then do we find our place, our function, our fulfillment, our personhood in Christ.

"Truly I tell you, just as you did it to one of the least of these who are members of my family, you did it to me" (Mt 25:40).

Many stories included an acute awareness of the need and brokenness of others, of injustice and echoed Gail's longing actively to help heal the brokenness or right the injustice.

Karen: I grew up in a segregated state. Blacks picked up the trash. I was five when I suggested, "Why don't we take the trash to her?" My dad agreed. We were not rich, but I remember the pain of crossing the road to that shantytown. God works through our early experiences—I felt then that I should be a missionary. I have never lost that awareness and continue to work in the area of social justice.

Nora: Looking at any kind of hurt too long will make you explode. We seem to have to reach out.

Joyce: When God shows me someone who needs help—food or comfort—I believe that God has put me there for a reason: to give that help as others have helped me.

Nora: Gail, how can it be that you have no scars or bitterness or even simple irritation at the things you have seen? If you give away just a little of the healed hands, the reconciled heart that you have, I'm sure you must save many.

Gail: Here is a song for you, because it is God who saves. You know, we just sing:

Lord of All

Dear Lord, we give to you our broken hearts,
    our broken lives, our broken dreams.
Our ships of pain we've built, embarked,
    and set to sail on empty seas.

Dear Lord, we give to you our deepest fears,
    the anguish of our darkest night,
Our scattered thoughts, our endless tears,
    our weary souls from restless flight.

Unto your table now we come,
Just as we are, Almighty King,
Knowing thou hast only love,
For every torn and broken thing.

Each shattered life you bid draw near,
    You take each piece to gently mend,
Each jagged edge, you file with care,
    'Til every heart is free again.

You take the pain, you take the fear,
    You give us peace and joy and light,
To you, there are no wasted years,
    You've paid the price; you've won the fight.

All glory be to thee, O Lord,
Creator of the great and small,
With you, we stand, we reign in life,
O Jesus Christ, you're Lord, Lord of all!

5

More Stories ✛

Behold how good and pleasant it is
   when sisters dwell in unity!
It is like the precious oil upon the head,
   running down upon the breast, upon the breast of Sarah,
   running down on the collar of her robes!
It is like the dew of Hermon,
   which falls on the mountains of Zion!
For there the Lord has commanded the blessing,
   Life for evermore.

Psalm 133 is a wisdom psalm celebrating the unity of the priests of Aaron. Here it has been rewritten for our gathering to speak in celebration of our unity as priests of Sarah.

As we told our stories—and laughed and cried and danced and ate together—we all became aware of this celebration of our unity, that supernatural bond Renée mentioned. The connecting threads in our stories were reflected in the connecting threads that grew between and among and around us—the intimacy, the shared identity. How often we found ourselves saying and writing "we" instead of "I." There was a sometimes frightening sense of losing our "I" and then finding it again in our "we." One woman wrote: "I am who I am. I am who we are. We are who we are. We are who I am."

Marilyn, writing about our time together, chose the same words and elaborated on them:

We are who we are—and the signs of who we are have been speaking to us from the heart of the Earth as we have sat together and talked and laughed and cried together.

Water lilies have blossomed at the edge of the river below the path we walk each day. The waxy beauty of the lily that sways gently with the flowing of the river reminds me of the beauty of each of the women I have met in the past few days. The beauty is there for all to see. But the sustaining life force that nourishes that beauty lies hidden beneath and is revealed only when one searches for it.

In our days together there have been companions of the Earth who have participated outside the window, acting out parables of the life being spoken in the room. I watched a little bird (don't ask its name) that worked diligently up and down the branches of the tree, moving all the way around, evidently as comfortable while walking upside down on the underside as it was walking right-side up. Within the room, the stories that were told reiterated this same skill of being able to function and cope with life, even when the world turns upside down.

One day a bird flew against the window pane, then bounced back, rolled over in the air and finally landed on a tree branch. The bird sat awhile, reeling back and forth, literally shaking its befuddled head. Inside, each of us continually flew into our own reflections in the stories of our sisters. And we too rolled off, feeling battered and confused.

As the week moved on, I have felt a growing sense of kinship with the river flowing by our door. The movement of the water and direction of the current is a paradigm of one of the major themes heard among us. In one way or another, we all expressed a need to see our lives as a movement with direction to it.

During break times there has been a great heaviness upon me, born out of that same reeling sensation that I saw in the bird that hurled itself so violently at its own reflection. This was a strange experience. At times I wanted to laugh and dance for joy. At times I would have liked to run and hide to avoid looking at the pain. There were moments when the urge to embrace was overwhelming. And sometimes sheer confusion drove wedges of distance between me and others.

For me, this has been a time in which the personhood of myself became lost in the power of the whole. I found myself living the life of each of *us*. It was frightening. There were times when it became necessary to run apart—almost as though the ME was being swallowed by the US. The "rugged individualist" in me is afraid of that.

Still, the joy of unity as women loved by God—and in love with God—draws us together. I think I have learned this week that one of life's paradoxes—for me—is this ambivalent yearning for closeness in love with others and a fear of loss of identity in the presence of that oneness ...

After our time alone for reflection and writing, we come together again to continue our stories. People arrive in twos and threes and settle into new places in the circle. Dianne, taking her turn to facilitate the group, collects us into silence and turns to Barbara whose turn it is to lead our gathering prayer:

Loving and beloved God,
Be with us as we gather in your name.
Open our ears to hear your word,
    to discover your grace in our lives.
Open our eyes to see your face in one another
    and to see the direction of your hand in our stories.
Open our hearts to your love
    and to each other as we speak and listen.
Bless us each with a taste of wisdom
    as we try to discern your will for us.
        AMEN.

Following the prayer Dianne looks from face to face to see who might be ready to speak next. Barbara smiles and nods: "I suppose it is my turn to speak as well as to pray." ...

Barbara

I have spent the past year mothering 33 children. Our home is a short-term emergency shelter for abused or neglected children who have nowhere else to go as well as those who have run away or are abandoned. I listen to my children's stories and wonder what small story I have to tell you when I hear in my head the stories of a 13-year-old prostitute, a sexually abused four-year-old, or a 16-year-old drug dealer.

I listen to these children and realize how blessed I was in my own parents. As a child I took their love—and God's love—for granted. I just knew that no matter how many terrible things I did, they would still love me. I tried not to do those terrible things because I knew that would hurt them. That is how I think about God now, too. I don't have trouble thinking of God as female, as one who loves me and accepts me unconditionally like my mother seemed to. I lean on that Mother-God love and struggle to pass it on to my children—to make my home a safe shelter for them where they feel accepted and cared for—no matter what. That is where God makes family out of my chaos, in loving me unconditionally—no matter what.

It feels rather like that here with you—a safe place where I am accepted, loved—no matter what. There is a sense of unconditional love and acceptance—of each other and of God's will. We disagree, but we don't judge; we become angry, but we still love! There is an intense and irrational maternal love here. I remember the birth of my first child as a profoundly spiritual moment, of being close to, in touch with, God. It was a moment of creation and wonder and of awestruck humility and sudden fierce and tender love—chaos and creation.

In the middle of my chaotic life, God somehow has created family and has caused love in places and ways that are beyond my imagination. I know this may sound simplistic and pious but it is not—I listen to my children, I look at my children, at each individual, incredibly unique face and I see a child of God, the face of Christ. I don't mean just the suffering, although that is there, too. I see the strength and the desire to love in spite of the pain. I see the wonderfully unique person that God has created in God's image. These children have taught me so much about love, about God.

And I will tell you another almost unbelievable story: Last Advent, at three in the morning, two police officers arrived at the door. As one handed me the bundle he carried and I looked in the blanket at a sleeping child of about nine months, the other said to my husband, who was trying to fill out the necessary papers, "I am sorry. We don't know anything at all about this baby right now. All we can tell you is his name ... 'Emmanuel.' "

Do not neglect to show hospitality to strangers, for by doing that some have entertained angels without knowing it (Heb 13:2).

Many of our stories included this openness to others, hospitality and an acceptance of their surprises and interruptions as gifts. Busyness was common in our lives and the "chaos" of which Barbara speaks often resulted in growth.

Grace: In many stories there is this ability of women to deal with so many levels of existence at the same time: family, self, leisure, work, study, church, society, God; and move so easily in and among those dimensions without any signs of schizophrenia.

Karen: In my story too, God has surprised me with people who are blessings to me. We thought we couldn't have children—I was told I was sterile "as a wooden door." In six months we received two babies for adoption. Three years later I was pregnant and had my first baby at 36. Six weeks after that baby was born, I was pregnant again. Now in addition to our growing family we have an unmarried pregnant teenager living with us. I understand the chaos and the blessing.

Renée: This womanly hospitality, this unconditional acceptance in Karen's and Barbara's stories, is happening here too. Maybe that is what women can offer the church—hospitality and acceptance that builds community.

The talk continues about women and community, about the women who have shaped our stories. A few bring cold drinks in from the kitchen and as we settle again Grace begins to speak, a slight Spanish accent enriching her rhythmic litany ...

Grace

I am the daughter of Dolores,
mother of three Marias and Flora,
granddaughter of Agneda and Roza, Leopoldina and Ana Maria,
sister of Shalom and Sue,
friend of Fatima and Analia,
cousin of Nedda and Ramonita,
and great, great ... granddaughter of Mary of Nazareth.

I do this because I feel my story intertwined with the spirit and life of many great women, near and far, present and past.

My mother's faith rested in Mary. She named me after Our Lady of Altagracia—"Grace from on high." I saw myself always as that, as grace. Through all my childhood experiences I felt and was that grace. It was natural to see myself wrapped in the life of God. I was never caught up in the same type of devotional life as my mother, but in my mind and my dreams I thought I came from and was made from God. My earliest prayers and dreams revolved around being with God.

Unlike my story and Terese's story, the church often forgets that we are to become like little children. I realize more and more now as I live with my own daughter, how unchildlike we are. This has become crucial to me—that the heart of the faith I hold is a child and a woman—Mary and her son. I am trying to understand my relationship to my mother and my daughter. For me a crucial issue in the church is understanding how we are all Marys incarnating the Word through Spirit.

My story has been one of grace and of dreams and of women who have inspired me, pushed me on, saved me, played with me, loved me.

"My soul magnifies the Lord" (Lk 1:46).

> *The idea that "we are all Marys incarnating the Word"*
> *—our own souls magnifying the Lord—generated a lively*
> *discussion; although some of us had difficulty identifying*
> *with Mary, nearly everyone's story included people—mostly*
> *women—who had in a real sense brought Christ to us. Our*
> *discussion of the role of Mary and the saints in our lives was*
> *an uncharacteristically tense moment in our gathering.*

Sandra: I am intrigued with Mary. It would be easier for me to try to be like Mary bringing Christ to others than to try to be like Jesus. But I can't pray to Mary like I can to Jesus.

Gail: I am uncomfortable with prayer to or through the saints. It bothered me when Helen put Hildegard in our prayer yesterday.

Anne: The saints are a comfortable part of my prayers. I ask for the prayers of the saints just as I would ask for your prayers. My prayer is to God, but I need the prayers of the community of saints past and present.

Susan: But prayer is for me that personal relationship with God. I don't know if I want people, even saints, in between.

Barbara: They are not "between," they are "with."

The tension and the misunderstanding becomes almost tangible as Nora begins to speak: "I think we need to pray."

> Lord, make me an instrument of your peace:
> Where there is hatred let me sow love
> Where there is injury, pardon
> Where there is doubt, faith
> Where there is ...

... "Help me, someone ... I've lost the words" ...
Three voices join hers as we continue:

Where there is despair, hope
Where there is darkness, light
And where there is sadness, joy.
   O Divine Master,
Grant that I may not so much seek
To be consoled as to console
To be understood as to understand
To be loved as to love.
For it is in giving that we receive
It is in pardoning that we are pardoned
And it is in dying that we are born to eternal life.
        AMEN.

The atmosphere is cleared. The topic is not closed—some of us continue the discussion on the walk to dinner, but the tone is different. We listen more easily.

When we return to our room by the water there is little hesitation about who will speak next. From the moment she walks into the room, the way in which she takes her chair captures our attention. Gabrielle has begun to speak to us before she has said a single word ...

Gabrielle

I am doing the questioning most people do before they are 25. Until recently I found no time for that questioning because I was immersed in marriage and babies and the earth—although I couldn't recognize the earth.

As a little girl I did not consider myself intellectually bright. I tried without questioning to do what was expected of me, even marrying the man my family and society channeled me toward instead of the man I really loved.

In one year I was faced with a combination of painful happenings—the death of my mother, my divorce and the murder of a child next door. As I worked through these griefs, I had to deal with my spiritual questioning. I began to claim my body through acting and dancing. The body/soul dualism of the church is difficult to overcome. I questioned the church and my faith. I am intrigued by the question, "How would we run the church as opposed to how men run it?" Just saying that stuns me—that they do run it.

I've lived my life surrounded by men, growing up with four brothers and then raising three sons. I should be an expert, but I have so many questions. I feel a constant sense of being judged by men that I don't feel with women. I question the hierarchy of the church, the sense the church gives me that God comes down to us from outside somewhere. I think of God coming up through people, out of their creativeness and relationships.

Women have been marginalized in the church; we have been neglected. But men too have unrealized parts of themselves that have been neglected.

Here we are learning from each other, recognizing God in each other, not looking upwards for God, not having our heads craned upward by the church. It helps us—and the church—relax. We can accept the good of the church more graciously.

She came to test him with hard questions (1 Kgs 10:1).

Our stories and our discussion produced many hard questions for ourselves and for the church. Questions about women and men, questions about the structure of the church, questions from the margins. Questions without easy answers, left open as challenges.

Elizabeth: Maybe it is being on the margins, on the outside, that allows us to question, to challenge. If so, the church will always need people on the margins and will need to listen to those prophetic questioning voices.

Grace: The questions in our stories are part of the profound, scrutinizing ways in which women look at their experiences.

Gabrielle: It seems that we love to examine our feelings and men like to give an opinion.

Helen: One of the traps I am learning to avoid is defining women in contrast to men—a kind of we are this way and they are that way arrangement that often ends in a value judgment, for instance, considering whether women are *more* prayerful than men. It is more productive to avoid considering what makes us different from men and rather search for what makes us most truly ourselves.

Caroline: Sometimes in discussions of women's spirituality I feel like an outsider because of my increasingly developed "male" traits, like analytical thinking. Being here helps me keep in touch with my female side and to keep a balance. Here we are promoting and celebrating what we consider to be a female method of operating. Feminism talks a lot about circular thinking, spirals and non-competitiveness—and it is important to bring these and other neglected modes of operating to the fore—but if we reject the "male" traits completely, I think we are in trouble. Matriarchy can be as sinful as patriarchy, and we are just as bad off if we become non-inclusive ourselves, excluding everything we are reacting against. I want to be "feminine" and I want to be "masculine" too. I think what we seek is balance—*both* analytic and circular thought, non-competitiveness and some healthy competition.

I seem to have a lot to say just now. Perhaps I should tell my story next ...

Caroline

As we tell our spiritual journeys, I am not so sure I want to draw a line between experience and spiritual experience. Having babies is a spiritual experience, so is changing dirty diapers, so is tasseling corn, playing the piano, running or making love. God is not only up or out there, but here in our lives, in our earth, our hearts, our minds, our blood. I do not mean to depersonalize God. I believe that God is a person, something other than everything, and yet is immanent and all around us.

As a little girl, I sometimes felt God's presence very near me. I remember writing poems about God in elementary school. When my mother taught me the Lord's Prayer I thought about it and lingered over every phrase when I prayed it to be sincere.

As a teenager I became disillusioned with my church and searched for another Christian community. I found a committed group for fellowship and Bible study and at age 15, before I realized what was happening, I became a full-fledged member of a destructive cult. Years later I was kidnapped and deprogrammed. At first I thought they were trying to take my faith away from me. Finally I realized that I had to go back to square one and question everything I believed. There was a period where I didn't think I believed and I was sad that I couldn't believe, but I always felt drawn back to the church.

I went to college and studied feminist theology. For many women feminism makes them draw away from the church, but for me it did the opposite. It redeemed the tradition for me. I began to feel that here was a way the tradition could again be meaningful for me.

As a seminarian, it has been refreshing to find myself able

to choose a particular tradition and embrace it wholeheartedly. It is not a prison for me, but a scaffolding on which to climb, a ground to stand on. Without it I couldn't make any journey.

There is no longer male and female; for all of you are one in Christ Jesus (Gal 3:28).

Repeatedly our relationship with the traditional church wove its way in and out of our stories. Many—but not all—of us struggled with integrating the issues raised by feminism with our traditions. We differed in the amount of change and renewal we felt was needed in the church, but all were in some way concerned that in "cleaning up" the tradition we not "throw the baby out with the bath water." Many of us presented a both-and rather than an either-or perspective.

Katie: Part of my experience has been not unlike Caroline's. I, who am so adept in the standard world at large (the masculine side some would say), quick to learn in the established structure of school, taking easily to organization, cataloguing and scientific processes, feel a little like a fish out of water here in this unorthodox, female setting.

Marilyn: We don't need to give up the masculine in order to celebrate the feminine, but it is hard to know what to do with the anger with which some of us respond to the oppression of patriarchy.

Katie: For me one of the most disturbing parts of this experience is the hostility toward men that I perceive under the surface. It troubles me that some women are so hurt that they cast their net of blame over an entire sex.

Anne: It is difficult for some of us to celebrate either the masculine or the traditional church when we are still feeling the oppression.

Karen: This experience which is common to so many of us—leaving the church for a period of time, searching and sorting, then returning with a fuller faith—suggests that the institutional church is oppressive to creative growth.

Terese: But there is strength to be found in the tradition, in the stories of the saints.

This is an ongoing discussion. We try to allow room for creative growth in our gathering. Instead of writing, some women choose to offer dramatic readings or dance. We rearrange our room as Gabrielle disappears to prepare for us a one-woman play. Another woman's story joins our own as we watch Meridel LeSueur's "The Girl" and are moved to tears and silence by the performance.

When we gather again, Dianne is ready to tell her story. She speaks as much with expression and gesture as with words ...

Dianne

Like Caroline, the tensions between feminism and faith have been central to my life. I think of myself as politically radical and religiously conservative. I throw myself into things totally. I live and love passionately.

Growing up I didn't fit the norm physically—I wanted to have blonde hair, blue eyes and small features. I only felt comfortable in my Greek Orthodox church where everyone looked like me. In graduate school I joined a small Russian Orthodox parish where every member counted and I felt needed. I got involved and it turned me around and was very good for me spiritually. I learned to live my faith.

But there was a conflict with my feminism which was so important to me at one point. I attended a conference for

Orthodox laity and returned to the parish really upset that
there was no grass roots movement in the Orthodox church
among women. I went through lots of outrage and pain then
and again later when my daughter started to ask questions.

Orthodoxy is very much a home thing. Home rituals are
important and always the women do that—special icons, incense, candles. Women can't help getting involved even if we
only do it for the children. Maybe that's why there's no big
movement to be in the liturgy because women have that involvement. I see God as loving, as very close to me and involved in my daily choices—small and large. Recently I decided
to go to law school and I felt that it would happen if that is
what God wants for me.

At one point I thought of leaving the church, but then I
would have to give up icons, lamb on Easter and all the traditions of my faith. I realized that this was part of my soul but
I had to reconcile Orthodoxy with my feminism. I feel that I
have learned about spirituality from women and about dogma
from men. I try to hold them together and somehow the
paradox of radical politics and conservative religion is where I
find myself whole.

I think that all of us have experienced compromise and
sacrifice. We have compromised our own beliefs and desires for
our families, our men, our church and society. Women know
what it is to be "a fool for Christ" in a way that men possibly
cannot understand.

We are fools for the sake of Christ (1 Cor 4:10).

*"Compromise and sacrifice." It is part of many of our
stories. Living with apparent contradiction, finding wholeness in paradox was also a common theme.*

Caroline: You have so much spirit! You are the perfect person for the task of wrestling with compromise and making life work. You even make those tensions sound fun.

Gabrielle: I am so encouraged by listening to you, Dianne. Most of us become frustrated by unfairness and obstacles and then we aren't effective at seeking change.

Dianne: We have something to show the church in our sacrifice for Christ. In a sense it is triumph, not defeat. I think men really expect women to be responsible for spiritual life. So I say, OK!

Nora: This business of living with compromise is an exciting thought, at least to me. Sometimes I think I'm standing still, squeezed between positions. It's probably not true at all. We need to have faith that what we do makes a difference, that there is a message in our lives, that there is power, even in acceptance ... or is that a capitulation again? When are we fools for God and when are we just fools?

Caroline: When we act in conscience, we are not fools. Some of us just act more visibly than others.

Dianne: I am still passionate about women's issues, political things, but I have realized that I can't change things tomorrow. I hope after law school to be an advocate for those who have suffered from injustice.

We talk about political involvement and issues of social justice. Karen speaks of a recent visit to Central America and begins to tell the story of Maria, a woman she met there ...

Maria

She sat crying softly. I was gathering my belongings, smelling the El Salvadoran bread I hoped to eat shortly. The chatter of us North Americans was aimless, reflecting a bit of our need for normalcy after the horror we had just seen through pictures and words given to us by a human rights group in San Salvador. It was as if we all saw the woman at once, because the chatter ceased and she began to speak in a very low, weak tone.

"I was captured by the national guard, tortured and taken to a hill where I was raped, stabbed, teeth knocked out and struck on the head." To assure us that she was telling the truth, she quietly lifted her blouse over her frail frame and revealed stab wounds under her breast. The anguish had not brought from her the information the guard had wanted—the location of her sons.

She recounted a litany of death and mutilation, which included all her brothers, sons and sons-in-law. The tears rolled down her cheeks as she recalled, "My daughter was seven months pregnant when she was picked up by the police. Her husband had already been killed and to this day she is 'disappeared.' " She modestly began to raise her skirt and on her stomach I could see the scars of gunshot wounds. "I was shot six times for asking about my daughter."

Her eyes moved around that warm room to connect with the 15 North American sets of eyes, all moist with shared pain. She concluded, "It's the truth I am telling you and that is the reason I am a member of the Mother's Committee of the Disappeared and Politically Assassinated."

As I put my arms around this my sister my words were so feeble, still she graciously accepted my offer of prayers. Our voices have been blending together since that day in 1985.

If one member suffers, all suffer together with it; if one member is honored, all rejoice together with it (1 Cor 12:26).

The room was wrapped in silence as we struggled with the immense emotion of that moment. Finally Barbara rose from the floor and moved in Karen's direction to offer an embrace. The silence was broken by waves of tears. When we eventually began to talk—about Maria and Karen and our responses to them—we explored what seemed the widest range of human feelings, from horror and pain and hate, to helplessness and despair, to anger, love, strength and justice. Maria's story is as indelibly marked on us as is any experience in all the years of our consultation.

Gail: We want to fight when we hear stories like Maria's. But this is the time when we must first go to Jesus for comfort. There is so much pain and we can give it to Christ.

Roberta: During trials and adverse conditions I am not complacent. I do not expect to sit idly by and rock my troubles away. My battle cry is that of the old spiritual I learned when I was young, "I'm a-gonna watch, fight and pray—until I die."

Joyce: Some of these world problems seem so out-of-reach. We can learn to handle what we can touch and make a difference for those we know, but out there ...

Nora: We women have a global dimension to our spirituality. Maybe men do too, but women seem to speak out more often from our personal experience to the world.

Social justice and political issues continue to weave through our discussion. Karen explains how she first became involved in Central America and shares her hopes for further international work. "Well, I'm telling my story already, so I may as well begin at the beginning." And she does ...

Karen

Both my mother and father were ordained ministers. In the

1950s it was not popular for one's mother to be off preaching, performing marriages that make the front page of a medium-sized city newspaper or being politically active. In was "in" to talk about how your mom was at the country club or about the latest fashion she designed for you to wear. And of course your mom was always at home preparing wonderful meals for everyone at whatever time they needed them.

It was not until college in the 60s that I truly valued the freedom from the norm my mother had given me. Listening to women trying to work through all their repressed desires for actualization, I realized my mother had already created the pattern, but I had been paralyzed with the cultural expectations and couldn't cut the cloth. What a release when I could finally celebrate instead of decry my childhood experiences!

This emancipation became a spiritual explosion when I realized God was a part of my new understanding. The compassion and the desire for social justice which had been in my heart since an early age could be expressed through me and—even more—should be expressed through me.

I married a minister and encountered cultural expectations again, not from him but from the many segments one finds in a parish. I have been rejected, questioned, maligned and at the same time admired, sought after for counsel and declared a role model for women. Walking in these two worlds has not been easy, but Mother cut the path for me, even at the expense of some childhood pain.

Women should dress themselves modestly and decently ... with good works, as is proper for women who profess reverence for God (1 Tim 2:9-10).

Mothers and daughters ... fathers and daughters ... wives

*and husbands ... girls and friends and women and friends
... women and their churches and their faith ... God as
father and as mother and as friend .... After Karen's story
and at many other times we explored the experience of
claiming for ourselves the woman we each were, sifting
through the influences on our formation and challenging the
expectations placed on women by both secular and religious
culture. What, after all, is truly "proper conduct" for
women of faith? We affirmed the need to reconcile expectations with self in order to become spiritually mature.*

Marilyn: For some of us here and for women all over, it has
been difficult to find helpful role models of women who lead
in church and religion. Look how we struggle with scripture's
restrictive passages on women. Karen, you really are blessed
with the experience your mother gave you. And we are blessed
too that you understood her and benefited from her presence.

Karen: Yet we all have women role models, some bold, some
more gentle. All our mothers have given us insight for our
spiritual journeys. My mother was just unique and ahead of her
time in matters of church. I'm thankful that I recognized that.

Renée: And yet you have a big family and do all those things
that I think of as traditional mothers' duties. I'm so impressed.

Susan: We all have such different talents. What we share is
the desire to do the right thing in the eyes of God and being
mature makes that task easier.

We enjoy a laugh about who has the distinction of being
most mature. Susan claims title, being the eldest and we defer.
After a short rest, we reassemble for the remaining stories.
Nora leans forward to acknowledge the invitation and with a
shrug of shoulder, begins ...

Nora

The reason I am here with you is that I'm an amateur analyst and a talker and someone heard me going on about differences between men and women one night at a meeting. That little tidbit says a lot about my life, really. I've not been one to set goals and draw maps to get to them. Life has been more an adventure for me and I guess I have trusted God would lead me. Mostly I don't "do" things; rather, things happen around me. My faith has always *been,* sort of without effort. Your references to the mystics and your familiarity with scripture awe me—I hardly get the newspaper read. And that is one of my goals.

I was raised in a fishbowl of sorts—a prominent family in the town. Mom was home, Dad was high profile. Our family life was strict and loving and a good Catholic experience. We had enough troubles to keep us humble. "God-fearing," Dad would call it. I behave in some ways like my mom, but those who know say that I am my father's daughter. I was always an interested student and went on right away for an M.A. I believe in the motto of my Benedictine women's college—"So Let Your Light Shine." A tension in my life is that I'm shining my light in a small space. I just couldn't go after the big time, there was always too much to do nearby. I don't know if that's wisdom or lack of courage. I do look at Karen with envy.

My husband and I had some years together before the children finally came and true to form, I have been home since … busy with volunteer things, but still home. Our little world has been rocked by friends' personal tragedies in recent years and my kitchen table has been privy to lots of coffee conversation. I've learned to listen better … all the sadness of my friends has made quite useless the words I love to use. There has been no time to wonder if I was on the right track—again, my job, it seems, is to be here, or there, or at the kitchen table.

This institute experience has been such a blessing for me. I don't take time to be alone or to pray really. We are very much together now, but I feel like it is almost alone for me—it is so peaceful. I believe this is a holy place and a holy experience. I love the kinship, the spiritual mix of faith and theology, the amazing flow of currents and crosscurrents in our stories. I depend on things happening for a purpose in my life; I believe we have a purpose here, perhaps more than we see now.

> *Rejoice with those who rejoice, weep with those who weep* (Rom 12:15).

> *Listening with compassion to others' pain happened not only at Nora's kitchen table but in other stories and in our time together.*

Helen: Nora, I don't think you give yourself enough credit. The work you do is important and it doesn't matter how others see its value. We are not all meant for the same work.

Nora: That's true and usually I am fairly comfortable with the way life is moving. But this is the time to discuss those things which distract us spiritually. Our youngest child gave me a gift the other day which I should share. I'd been gone and when he saw me back home and at the kitchen sink, he ran up to give me a hug and said, "Moms are for hugs because hugs give kids life." I laid my utensil on the counter and wrote the line on my grocery list. And then I cried.

We talk about how much we cry, about the tears and the ache that seem so close to the surface much of the time, about both the grief and the joy that sometimes consume us. But the melancholy mood doesn't last long. Karen repositions the tissue box amid the clutter of the table, we lean back collectively into sofas and chairs and turn our attention to Helen, whose thoughtful look tells us she is ready to speak ...

Helen

This year I became aware that I have an eating disorder. I was battling stress and used food to combat this. I have had a demanding executive position and I finally went to Overeaters Anonymous and learned about the Twelve-Step Program of AA. I saw it as an overall pattern for my whole spiritual life. I have spent my whole life on diets. In eighth grade I weighed 150 pounds and I have never weighed less. I have frequently dieted to lose weight but the stress would start and I'd go off the diet. Last year at OA they said, this is a disease. Part of this I hated, part was a relief. Could I forgive myself for this?

I went to a dependency center for treatment. I had no idea of the amount of pain this would cause me. I had always been in control and I realized I had to let go. It is so hard for me to get in touch with my feelings but they said I'd never get well if I didn't. I could do everything else—why not this? I had never stopped long enough to feel much. It took 13 weeks. Every diet before this said, "get control of yourself!" This time I had to learn that I was really powerless. I had to give my life over to God.

I thought that I had done this when I took my monastic vows. I thought then that if God is really what everyone says God is, I can't help but submit. Now I see that I had learned the language of surrender, but I was really still in charge—still in the driver's seat. I had to admit this time that I could not do that. I had to really turn my life over to God.

I lost 50 pounds and it was not difficult. I just had to let God do it. I once thought it was just language, but it does work. I learned about how harsh I'd been with myself and how much gentler I needed to be. By accepting my weakness, I've become strengthened. In this weakness is my strength. My connection with the human race is in my brokenness.

Let go and let God. It is when I stopped trying to be in control, when I really surrendered, that I was truly empowered in myself and in my faith. It has turned me around spiritually, made me more vulnerable and open to God. My prayer life is now more contemplative—more waiting and listening. I am also less controlling and more open to people in my daily life. I feel a radical dependence on God and it is in that dependence that I am free.

Trust in the Lord with all your heart (Prov 3:5).

Let go and let God. We talked often about control and surrender, about vulnerability and dependence.

Katie: Helen, your story shows how patient God can be. God never seems to use force, but waits until you're ready. At that point God helps out. That is what good parents do.

Helen: Before therapy, I prayed to God, "Help me to do this." In the middle I thought, "Not this much!"

Roberta: I don't give in to my physical deficiencies, but they have taught me to leave it in God's hands. I have learned to depend more on God, to relax and let go. Things work out.

Caroline: Perhaps because we as women have traditionally had less control of our own lives, this surrender comes more naturally for us.

Helen: I have found that contemplative prayer has helped me to let go, to surrender my control and to rest in God as I did as a child.

Gail: Surrender walks hand in hand with trust. The Lord will teach us if we allow it.

Gail begins to sing ...

Teach Us to Fly

Dear Lord, teach us to fly on your wings
   of surrender and trust,
To rest in your hands gentle Father,
   for thou art the potter,
   to thee we abandon ourselves
As clay must.

To be centered and soaked, to be trimmed, to be turned,
   to be dried ... set aside.
And when cracked, to be crushed into slip,
   to be pugged, to be stripped
Of all strength and pride.

To be fired and fired, higher and higher,
Then how, no one knows,
Made meet for the Master's use,
A vessel of gold.

Make us vessels of gold.

6

Worship ✦

I have arrived at the common room of the institute early, before all the others, to have some time alone with the water before our final worship service together. The evening is still, but the water is alive, moving. The lake outside is really part of a chain of lakes that surfaces and goes underground again, individual parts of a secretly connected river. Mirrored in its surface I see individual women, separately alive, flowing together underground. There are springs here, too, in front of our window, flowing, renewing the lake, the river ... and us.

The silence is broken by laughter—children in a canoe on the other side of the water. A great blue heron flies overhead. It has been good here, with the women and the water, but I have missed my children. It will be good to be home. I wonder what memories I will take home with me from here—these women, their faces, their voices.

I hear the door behind me and turn to greet the women whom in such a short time I have come to love. Elizabeth and

Renée arrive together. Although they are not alike, they look like mother and daughter as they talk together; sometimes it is not clear which is mother and which is daughter. There is a liveliness, life-growing, between them that is almost tangible.

The others trickle in, some in silence, some laughing or talking quietly together. The greetings are mostly wordless—a touch, a smile. I watch the women's faces and their hands. Something has changed here. As we have grown together I have seen these faces—the smiles, the tears, the glimpses of subtle transient emotion, the startling clarity of eyes that love and understand; I have watched these hands—gently expressive, speaking with touch or gesture words that elude the mouth. And I have learned to observe with new eyes. Each woman—an individual face, unique hands, the shape of a mouth, the curve of a cheek, the dance of a finger—has grown inexpressibly beautiful to me. A transfiguration. The radiance of the faces fills the room. Yes. It is true. We are made in God's image.

We sit in a circle, some on cushions on the floor, a few on chairs. Gathering comfortably, we look around the circle from one face to another, aware of a bond linking us. The children's laughter can still be heard. It is good, bell-like, calling us together. Gail begins to sing, her voice clear and gentle, "Morning has broken like the first morning ... " Gradually we join in.

We are silent a moment before joining together in a prayer of confession:

> Creating God in whose image we were made, you know full well our limitations and our weaknesses which open the door for sin. We humbly confess to you that we have failed to keep the wideness of your love before our eyes, and so have lost patience with ourselves and others.

We have turned from our trust in you and as a result have been anxious about our future.

We have failed to keep the cross of Christ always before us and thereby allowed feelings of condemnation to enter in.

We have felt an aching in our hearts for you, but have turned to people and things to fill this void.

Forgive us, Lord, in your mercy which envelops us like a mother's love. By your Holy Spirit draw us closer to you that the light of your wisdom might shine more brightly in our faces, and the melody of your love resonate in our souls. In the name of Christ our Savior we pray. AMEN.

After a period of silent prayer and the assurance of pardon we sing together "Come down O Love Divine." We shift from the circle to a more "standard" worship setting facing the small table in the chapel-like side alcove under the skylight.

Susan, her well-worn Bible in hand, stands in front of our semicircle of chairs and reads, "In the beginning God created the heavens and the earth ... ." We listen to the first chapter of Genesis. Dianne in turn reads from Ezekiel—the valley of the dry bones (37:1-10): " ... I will cause breath to enter you and you shall live ... ." And Terese reads the first eight verses of the third chapter of the Gospel of John: " ... The spirit blows where it wills, and you hear the sound of it, but you do not know whence it comes or whither it goes ... ."

Caroline, looking very young—and at the same time very wise—moves to the front of the group and begins to speak:

"In the beginning God created the heavens and the earth, the earth was without form and void, and darkness was upon the face of the deep; and the Ruach of God was moving over the face of the waters."

These are the words which open the creation narrative in Genesis. The story which follows recounts God's action as a planned, orderly progression. God calls something into being, and it is. God calls to the light, "light" and there is light. God says "Let there be a firmament in the midst of the waters," and it is so. Everything proceeds as planned.

This creation account leads us to believe that when God acts, God acts in an orderly, planned progression in which there are no mistakes, no rough drafts, no wasted energy, and no diversions which lead away from the main goal.

But if we go back to the beginning of the story, we hear another voice about the nature of God's creative activity: the Spirit of God was moving over the face of the waters. The presence of God's spirit, the Ruach, the wind, is a necessary precondition for God's creation.

When we set out to tell our life stories, we somehow expected that they, like the creation of the world, should proceed along a neat, orderly progression. As Karen said earlier this week, we expect that there is some *place* we are aiming toward, that we will get there and remain there for the rest of our lives. Instead we find the journey of our lives is circuitous. It is not a paved road between two destinations, but a collection of trails and paths, often in wooded areas where we cannot see beyond the next bend. Life is full of paths that seem to intersect and bring us around to the same places again, but that are seemingly leading nowhere in particular.

To use another metaphor and take you down to the waterfront, our lives do not proceed like an ocean liner steadily moving from one continent to another. Life is more like sailing. And God enters our lives as the Ruach, the spirit, the wind moving over the face of the waters.

The wind is not something tangible. "The wind blows where it wills, and you hear the sound of it, but you do not know whence it comes or whither it goes." We cannot grasp the wind in our hand. We cannot see it or taste it. We only know its presence in the rustle of the leaves, in its refreshing coolness on our skins, or in the ripples across the face of the lake. We know the wind only by its effects.

The wind is free, it comes and goes as it pleases. There are times when it blows generously, but there are times when we must wait for hours or even days, our sails hanging limply from the mast.

Sailing is not the most efficient means of transportation. It is not the quickest way to move from point A to B. The sailor is at the mercy of the wind. She must wait for its coming and its going. She must adjust herself to the changes in its direction. So the sailor does not always sail in a straight line but tacks back and forth, back and forth, in order to catch the wind at the proper angle to move her ahead. The sailor sails for the sheer pleasure of sailing, for the thrill of the dance between the wind and vessel—a dance in which the wind leads, and the vessel follows. In the beauty of that union, a journey is made. It is the journey itself—the dance and the union—that is as important to the sailor as the destination.

The notion of spirit as wind is too unpredictable for many of us. Sometimes the wind comes when we do not want it. Sometimes it does not come when we are desperately longing for it. But eventually it does come. So, like the sailor, we must be ready for it, waiting with our sails trimmed, waiting to let the spirit take us where it wills. Only by giving ourselves to the spirit can we become sleek and graceful sailing vessels. The sailor's trade demands of us the willingness to let go. We are also called upon to have courage, because our navigational maps are only provisional. Many of the waters in our life are uncharted.

We often think of spirit in opposition to the flesh. Even in scripture the two are juxtaposed as polar opposites. I suggest we think of the spirit and of that which has physical being as complementary to one another. The wind, the Ruach, is not recognized except in the physical manifestations of its presence, in the leaves, the ripples on the water, in the sails that billow out from where they are held. Just as the spirit is recognized in the manifestation of its presence, so the lump of clay called "adam," that is, "the human," is not animated until it has received the breath of life.

We find we need not only the leading of the spirit, but the bones of our tradition and our church as well. The bones, the church and its tradition, are the vessel for the spirit. But, like the dry bones of Ezekiel, without the spirit the bones lie useless in the dust. The church has always struggled with this dialectic between flesh and spirit, between the bones and the breath of life. When courage is lacking, we no longer let ourselves go to the leading of the spirit, but instead *cling* to the safety of our tradition—to what we can see and feel and touch, to what is predictable and safe.

It may cross your mind that this is an accusation more properly levelled against our *brothers* in Christ. We see the spirit leading the women of the church in new directions, leading us to speak of God with female imagery and to change our thinking about sexuality, or to question the wholeness of the scriptures we hold so dear. In all this it appears the men are the ones clinging to the dusty old bones of an outdated tradition. But a similar temptation comes for us as women, only in a different disguise.

We as women are moving into uncharted waters, *beyond* what is now considered "tradition". With that comes the fear that if we sail too far, we may fall off the end of the earth. To put it more directly, when our experience leads us to go against what the church teaches, it is easy to let ourselves be condemned and say, "I must not be a good person," or "I must not be right in the eyes of God" because there is a particular church teaching that says so. But the bones without the spirit have no life. If we give in to this temptation to feel condemned by God and not loved, then we either resist the new directions the spirit is leading us in, or we walk away from the tradition altogether.

To let ourselves go with the leading of the spirit calls for courage. I believe God is calling us as women to have the courage *not* to let ourselves be condemned—to DARE to believe that God loves us and forgives us, that God will save us, even when the church accuses us of straying from the fold. God is doing a new thing with her people; through women everywhere, God is breathing life into dusty old bones. Let us have the courage to be led into new, uncharted waters, and to trust in God's unfathomable love.

We are silent together for a while.

Marilyn gathers us into a circle again around the small table. God's peace is among us, a blessing. Marilyn presides at God's table and we share communion, passing the bread and the cup from one to another around the circle—a time of thanksgiving. "Eucharist" means thanksgiving.

And we sing:

Come to the mountain top,
Leave all your cares behind,
He spoke so gently to me.
Lay all your burdens down,
Such peace and joy you'll find,
Come take my hand and you'll see.

You will ... fly, fly, fly like a butterfly,
    gliding on wings of the wind,
Never having to hide deep inside your cocoon,
    once again.

Look, world look all around me,
    my chains are gone, I know I've been set free.
I'm safely resting in Jesus again.

I listened quietly,
    He waited patiently,
He didn't push, didn't shove.
I gave him my sorrows,
Today's cares, tomorrow's,
And he wrapped them up in his love.

He said ... fly, fly, fly like a butterfly,
    gliding on the wings of the wind,
Never having to hide deep inside your cocoon,
    once again.
Look, world, look all around me,
    my chains are gone, I know I've been set free.
I'm safely resting in Jesus again.

Now I can ... fly ...

7

Meditations ✢

Someone notes, "I'm afraid this little writing project has produced more questions in my mind than answers."

At each of our gatherings we wrote personal reflections in addition to telling our stories. At one time or another each of us tried to write conclusions and found instead more questions. Often we were comfortable with the questions, suggestions and speculations. The Spirit blows where it will and we accepted it. As Terese wrote, "One thought becomes a dozen questions, so I am going to turn this all over to my heart and the Holy Spirit."

Our writings reflect the multiple languages of our gathering—the stories, the feelings, the settings, the struggles, the prayers and laughter, movement and stillness and song. We reflected on common subjects, but from our unique perspectives. With the written reflections, as with the original idea, there was neither planned agenda nor argument nor specific direction: the patterns and movements were spontaneous.

In a letter to us at the end of one summer, Patricia commented on the leadership dynamic of the group, which was as fluid as the flow of ideas:

The old lines, "Don't walk ahead of me, I may not follow; don't walk behind me, I may not lead; just walk beside me and be my friend" are nice, but often may not move anyone anywhere. There are times when I need to be led (maybe even dragged kicking and screaming) and times when I can't help running ahead (friends ought to follow me to be sure I don't get lost). It is good to have been in a situation where I could follow you without feeling my integrity—my faith—was threatened; and good to feel free to move in the direction I was going without feeling I had threatened you. Many people have described women's leadership as circular rather than hierarchical and I always thought of the circle as flat, rather like ring-a-round-the-rosy. It seems we're more dynamic, like a Ferris wheel (with different people at the top at various times) or perhaps a carousel with everyone taking turns going up and down.

At times the ride was dizzying, at times slow, but always there was movement and growth. Join the ride with us and listen to the voices.

A primary subject of our reflections was love:

... What struck me as special to our group was the acceptance of each person's individuality, of differentness. There was unconditional love. No one was loved for what they did, but for who they were (something I am still trying to get used to). It was unjudgmental but not necessarily uncritical—although somewhat that too. (Caroline)

... I have never felt such gentle, motherly acceptance as I have through this experience. (Terese)

... My image of God changed here ... The God I experienced at the institute was different than the God I was getting to know at school. The boundaries of my tradition became much more flexible here. Does God really care so much about rules? When I heard Gabrielle and Elizabeth speak, I did not feel like condemning them, saying "Well, correct doctrine says you're wrong so you have to learn to be something that you aren't." Rather when I heard them speak, I loved them, I wanted to wipe their tears away and tell them that it was all right. I felt such love for them. If I loved them so much, how much more does God? (Caroline)

Some of us asked, "What of love and the church?"

... Unconditional love and acceptance. It has been missing in many parts of the church in my life, but present in the church experienced in my case through women. We as Christians, as women, need it, but where do we get it? (Barbara)

... We talked about so much and the common themes are not new to the male-made church—death and grieving, birth and life, our butterfly's resurrection. But our way of meeting them seems new—unconditional love and acceptance, of each other and of God's will. As Barbara said, we disagree, but we don't judge, we become angry, but we still love. We accept movement in circles and cycles, not linear and progressive. Not leading in a line but dancing in a circle. (Anne)

... This God loves us the way that we are. It does not mean that God does not call us to be more than we are at this moment. That is just the point. God calls us, God does not push, shove and squeeze. (Caroline)

... Because of this unconditional love or acceptance, we feel safe with God and with each other. (Sandra)

We felt safe with one another and in safety we found growth:

... Never in my life have I felt so safe, it was possible to spill the entire contents of my soul onto a table to be closely examined by others whom I had only known for a day. (Katie)

... I have to agree with Gabrielle that "I am comfortable enough to humiliate myself." (Dianne)

... The warmth and love present in the room as each of us shared our deepest secrets was almost tangible. I felt so secure and at home with you, it's like having a second family. (Renée)

... And I, whose faith experience does not include a "personal relationship" with Jesus, nor any great moment of grace or communion with the Holy Spirit—felt touched, guided, made holy, protected by the presence of the Holy Spirit in our community. I found myself feeling safe. (Nora)

... There was a vivid sense of prayer as a relationship with God and a feeling of communion among us. In our relationship with God, we are each somehow part of each other. (Barbara)

... I was deepened in my awareness of how I thrive and grow in the comforting circles of women's presence. I am at home with them. I don't rehearse my words. I don't feel competitive. The roominess and support I feel with women comes closest to the feeling of safety and unconditional love I feel coming from God, my mother/father. (Helen)

And we arrive back at unconditional love. Why is this experience so comforting?

... I wonder what has made us feel so safe here. How is this different from other groups of women, groups of Christians, or support groups? (Sandra)

... Prior to attending this conference, I'd gone to two other meetings where the role of women in the church was the main topic of discussion. The climate of those deliberations was tense and, in my view, not productive. Justifiable or not, many of the women expressed anger and hostility toward the church and other women who did not share their views. I was dismayed at what I had seen and heard. (Roberta)

... We women, here at least, want to accommodate, to assimilate, to attend to one another's ideas even when we don't agree intellectually. (Nora)

... Somehow there developed quickly a sincere feeling of respect for one another and a deep concern for each other. There was an open-mindedness as we heard with interest of our different approaches and experiences. (Susan)

... But what makes this different: Our stories? Our agenda —or lack of one? Our times of prayer and worship? (Anne)

... One thing we have seen here is growth through affirmation. Jesus exampled that, our personal experiences exampled that and yet the traditional institutional experience has been growth through fear and judgment. (Karen)

... It seems we all struggle with our traditions. Here we are promoting and celebrating what we consider a female method of operating. It is important in the church and in the wider culture to bring these neglected modes to the fore, but if we reject the "male" traits completely, I think we are in trouble. What we seek is balance—BOTH instead of either/or. (Caroline)

We are turning again to thoughts about the tensions between faith and church.

... The traditional church, its structure and way of doing things, has often saddened me—not in a male or female sense, but because we are so clothed in the garment of the world. I'm not sure that if I could, I would change structure in the church —male to female, female to male. I would change hearts. (Gail)

... It's with our hearts, not our heads, that we have been telling our stories. We have spoken not of structure, or rules, but of our lives. Jesus too spoke of life rather than law. (Barbara)

... Jesus was always processing life stories. In fact, the disciples would want to talk about issues philosophically and Jesus would abruptly bring them back to life stories—the woman with the lost coin, the woman with the flow of blood, the woman grinding at the mill. (Karen)

... We look carefully at the biblical stories as we do at our own. What is apparent here is the profound and scrutinizing ways in which women look at their experiences. (Grace)

... I love the intensity of the women here with me. (Gabrielle)

Intensity and passion. We examine the personal dimensions of faith, discovered through story:

... Even more apparent is the gift of compassion. Every story showed the empathetic nature of women toward the suffering, the needy, the less fortunate ones. This compassion is for me the key to living out the central message of the Gospel to feed the hungry, clothe the naked, free the prisoners. (Grace)

... And Jesus says that the needy one is he himself. (Susan)

... We need desperately to keep the activity/ministry of the church personal. Many programs for the needy are so impersonal, cold and efficient there is no opportunity in them to feel the reverence that should be ours if Jesus is the one being served. (Grace)

... Just as my relationship with God is very personal, my relationship with God's people is that way, too. (Susan)

... For me it is personal, too. I am a good friend and try to help those in difficulty. I am honest and sometimes I speak too soon. People don't always like to hear the truth. (Joyce)

... Hearing the truth is hard. One of the most sobering parts of this experience for me, was being drawn out of my protective, suburban environment to hear stories told by average middle-class Americans that were frankly traumatic. (Katie)

The stories as life and life as prayer:

... Each life story carries with it the moments of struggle and tragedy, as well as the moments of celebration and self-discovery. There seems to be a general sense of spiritual reaching out to grow in relationship with God and with one another as women. In a sense each one of us came bringing a living book of adventure, romance, dreams and drama. (Marilyn)

... We tend to see the difficult and painful happenings of our lives as ways in which we have been called anew by God. They seem to show that God is faithful and persistent. (Helen)

... Our stories exemplified the opportunity that comes out of crisis if we can cling to the thread of hope, or of my favorite symbol—the phoenix rising from the ashes of despair. (Elizabeth)

... As we told our stories of God's presence in our daily lives, we grew to a better understanding of our work as sacred, as prayer. (Joyce)

... For some of us our spirituality is expressed more in our work and ideas than in our prayer life. (Nora)

... The physical and spiritual seem to belong together. Crying, singing, praying, celebrating, arguing—we do these things comfortably with one another and with God. (Anne)

... Many of our life stories show a conviction that happiness consists of very simple things. We heard that thought in the final line of Gabrielle's performance from "The Girl"—"Oh, it's good to live. You don't have to have much, just to know each other, touch, sing, feel in your breast and throat." (Helen)

... I have no doubt that each person in the group is a chosen woman, a holy person, a gift to the world as unique and as precious as any hero, priest or prophet. How great if we, convinced of our uniqueness and chosenness, could persuade those who don't believe in themselves that they too are chosen and that each of us is here as divinely as anyone is here. (Grace)

... What matters most is just to reach out and love and be real. (Gail)

... So often we seem to see God as a friend, companion, parent, very near and caring about even our most personal, mundane, minute concerns. I'm particularly curious to see if God seems more distant for men and less involved in their lives. If this were true, then we could say that what women in particular have to offer is a more present sense of God being there—being a constant companion. (Caroline)

What do we women in particular have to offer to our communities of faith? Have we learned something here?

... To answer the question of what we as women could give to our churches or communities that seems to be missing, I think it is our strong sense of hospitality. We can give our love, our warmth and our acceptance and make our churches into what I have always thought a community should be: something people belong to that offers them unconditional love and a true sense of security from others they can trust. (Renée)

... This Christian community is also a model for friendship and communication: love and respect rule here and both differences and likenesses are celebrated. I see us as one, as catholic really, with differences of dogma, sacrament and worship, but with the likenesses of faith and trust in God. We pursue our commonness of faith but avoid judgment. There must be a way to transfer this experience to groups of Christian people elsewhere. Just as we want to foster the feminine experience of God alongside the masculine experience, so we should also seek to build networks for interfaith community. (Nora)

... I hope we've uncovered a truth here—when we give each other the chance to tell our stories, bonds are formed, understanding is forged despite age-old religious differences. (Gabrielle)

... The experience has confirmed that "this tradition is where I belong" but we also feel like other traditions have a place too—for they guard other aspects of the Christian tradition. (Joyce)

... The sense of community, of church, has been powerful here. The God we pray to has been the same God for us all— the loving, just, compassionate God whom we struggle to identify with words. (Terese)

We wrote sometimes of being at ease with our God, at other times of being restless in the Lord:

... I think a relationship with God is not something to be forced or rushed. It needs to develop on its own. (Katie)

... Most of us spoke easily about seeing God's hand in our lives and being able to accept disappointments and setbacks— seeing losses as opportunities for new life. (Terese)

... I have always felt God put each of us in a certain place at a certain time. This thought was with me often during our time together. (Joyce)

... I think our tolerance of individuality helps us to understand who God is, because we are all made in God's image.

When individuality is squelched, then part of God's nature must be hidden in the process. (Caroline)

... Human beings need the tensions that come from living with differences—as long as there is love. (Nora)

... This restlessness in the Lord is a gift to us and to the church. When we are certain we have God figured out, then we have made God into our own image and likeness. We must cultivate this restlessness, this searching, this longing for God's face, for knowledge of God's plan and design for us. (Grace)

... Looking around I see faces with such concern—shadows of God. This is data. This is how God loves us—eyes full of love. I can see a circle of love. (Helen)

In this circle we talked about our writings and later some of us continued to write. What Elizabeth wrote blessed us all on our way:

In setting the scene for my writing I need to look out at the calm, cool rippling water. I feel one with it—so clean and pure. I have discarded any physically constricting clothing, washed my face and even brushed my teeth and I'm now wearing a large and roomy blue, gray and white cotton shift. I feel as if in this past week I've been going through a rite of passage—a purification, a renewal, a rebirth—and when I leave here I truly will go with newly grown wings.

Looking out at the water seems to soothe me as the voices and touches and smiles and tears of the women here have done. The greenery before me in the trees! How can there be so many shades of green? The women here! How can we be so different and so much the same?

As women we seem to share some special mysteries. Who would have imagined that we could bond as we have? That first night we met we began to dance, peeking out from under our masks a bit to introduce each other. Over the days we have been choreographed closer together in our dance through the common language of our experiences. Not that we have had the same experiences but we seem to have been able to draw from the history of "herstory" to know each other's story—almost, for the moment, as if it were our own.

Never before have I experienced this long a period of time with "just" women—women's bodies, smells, voices, energy, expressions and language. The women's language we talked about earlier seems to draw from an ancient spring of voices.

I had felt like a female bird that couldn't fly. With the kind, gentle, loving encouragement to help me—and with my God—I found wings. Women here cared enough to try to understand this strange bird. My heart and my spirit grew with this sensitivity, sympathy and understanding. My wings are still small, but I have WINGS. New life has been breathed into me by each of you and soon our flock of beautiful birds will fly each in a different direction—together.

> *Dear Lord, teach us to fly on your wings*
> *of surrender and trust ...*

8

Search ✛

Rekindle the gift of God that is within you (2 Tim 1:6).

What gifts, what blessings, have we given ourselves?
What gifts, what blessings, can we offer the church?

The work of our gatherings was two-fold: to tell our stories and to interpret them. Because we soon learned to trust one another with our stories, the interpretations became our challenge. What were we to do with what we were hearing from one another and from the voice within? Journeying through the process from year to year, we gradually absorbed the meaning of our experience and devised a plan to articulate this ...

As I pull my coat closer to shut out the Minnesota snow, these questions dance in my thoughts, calling up warm memories of Minnesota summer. The natural world was so much a part of our experience: walking together by the lake, lounging in the cool grass, drinking in the sunshine. The natural world was so much a part of our time together that it seems odd to be meditating on those summer thoughts here in the cold. Yet the thoughts thrive in the dancing snow. Several of us are meeting for lunch in the fall after our second summer, hoping to pull together the experiences and the discussions from our times together at the Ecumenical Institute: What really happened those summers? What did we learn? Where are we to go next?

Coming into the sandwich shop from the cold, my glasses fog over and I am hugged by three women before I can even see them. Blindly I recognize the voices, the hugs and the laughter. The reunion is good. We eat and talk and the story continues. We tell of happenings in our lives great and small and we reminisce about our summer gatherings, about blessings given and received. Karen, the facilitator, reads us our "committee prose"—the consensus statement we wrote after the first year: "We as women have observed some common themes in our spiritual experiences that have not been recognized or expressed in the dominant understanding of Christian spirituality." Oh yes! We begin to elaborate. Listen ...

"These connecting threads in our stories—what we have in common in our experience as women, as Christians, things that haven't been expressed in our church, that are with us here and that have made our time together what it is—they will be our gift to each other and to our church." ...

"As we met together, we soon came to realize that what we were really trying to articulate were *not* those qualities that made us different from others, but those qualities that made us *most truly ourselves.* I have had difficulty considering how and why women and men differ from each other in regard to spirituality. A more honest approach is to consider those qualities in women's spirituality that make us most truly ourselves." ...

"A sharing of faith experiences produced a better understanding of the faith lives of women, one that transcended generations and denominations. Among the group there seemed to be a universal appreciation of the feminine qualities and the particular gifts women bring to the church. There was a strong sense of ownership of feminine values and unanimous objection to becoming more 'male' in our attempt to reach the full measure of equality." ...

We struggle together trying to capture those elusive "feminine values" or "shared themes" that were expressed more often as shared images than as concepts. We make lists of themes and images that recurred frequently in our stories. The list grows: some expected themes, some surprises and some we all seem to recognize but cannot express. Listen to a few of the suggestions we toss on the table:

"*Childhood experiences*—many of us trace our spiritual journey from them; 'when I was a little girl' is an important part of who we are—it is not just an imperfect adulthood."

"And there is also a *naturalness of faith in God,* almost taking it for granted, without needing reasons, accepting a continuity of faith, without huge leaps and giant steps."

"That is paired with *an awareness of God,* a sort of continuing consciousness, a close to the surface questioning—what does God want of me?"

"Maybe that is part of *the search for 'most truly ourselves'*."

"There seems to be a *common language among women.* So often it seems communications that are clear between women (often of a spiritual nature) are baffling to men."

"So often our stories run into *limits*—we are limited by institutions outside our lives and interruptions within our lives, by cultural expectations and by family expectations."

"Yes. And similarly we face *marginalization,* feeling on the sideline or unimportant."

"There seems to be a pattern of *valuing relationships over ideas;* we tend to identify and define ourselves by associations."

"Often in our stories the issue of *perfection* came up."

"There seem to be two sorts of perfection: First, a striving to meet the expectations of others, of society, of the church, of ourselves; often this is accompanied by the message that we don't or can't meet those expectations. Second, a search for spiritual purity—an attempt to grow more perfect in love."

"We see patterns of *circles and cycles* rather than linear development in our life stories and there are similar patterns of leadership in our groups."

"In our stories and especially evident in our gathering together there was often a sense of *unconditional love,* of hospitality, an acceptance of others without questioning or trying to change or convert or control them."

"We seem generally *uncomfortable with control,* an implication that control is unhealthy. There is a corresponding willingness to relinquish control, to *let go and let God*—a recognition of the truth: in whose service is perfect freedom."

"There is a willingness to be *vulnerable* to others and God."

And on and on. The list grows and somehow as we attempt to be more specific the list becomes more vague. Variations on related themes intertwine and repeatedly we return to faith and awareness of God, which cannot be tied down. We put the list aside and order dessert. We talk some more and bless each other on our separate ways. It is still snowing. The themes and patterns are swirling in my head like the snowflakes. I know, I just know, there is some pattern here I cannot see. The circles and cycles are twisting themselves into some sort of tapestry woven out of our common life stories. What is it after all that is important here?

The process is holy.

I hear the words. I don't know which of us voiced them; perhaps it was I. I know that it is true. I know also that it answers our question about the blessing that we have received, that we want to offer to others. The process is holy ... the process is the gift, the blessing.

It is summer again. We are together beside the lake; even the great blue heron has returned to greet us. I listen to the stories, look at the faces of these women I have grown to love and see that we are blessed by what has happened to us, among us. What is important here is what is happening, even if we cannot precisely articulate what it is and how it has happened. The process is holy.

One voice suggests: "I suspect the gift we have to share with men and articulate for ourselves and for them has not so much to do with essential themes of religion or life (death, grieving, uncertainty, love) which are probably universal, but with the way we approach or deal with those themes."

This thought becomes a theme for our third summer discussion. Our consultation report prepared for a meeting of the institute board confirms:

"Perhaps even more important than our themes is the *process* itself. This process creates a safe, loving atmosphere that allows for a sharing of spiritual stories and gifts—a process that may facilitate healing between men and women in the church."

How do we explain what has happened here? We look again at the process—at what we found here at the Ecumenical Institute and at what we brought to it ourselves.

"Do not fear, only believe" (Mark 5:36).

I came to the first meeting full of apprehension. I was nervous, skeptical, curious and defensive. I had made all the arrangements to leave my family for the full five days, even though I lived nearby and the exercise of packing and bidding good-bye seemed unnecessary and contrived. I told myself I was honoring a commitment, that the good hosts at the institute could be trusted and that it would soon be over ... but, truly, it will never be over.

I participated in the introductory activity of that first gathering, although I kept myself at a safe distance. Having sized everyone up to my initial satisfaction, I engaged in the cumbersome post-session small talk and then withdrew to my monk-like room in one of the living quarters on the institute grounds. Well, I thought, I'll stay the night and reassess in the morning.

Morning passed easily. I sensed that it was good for me to be there. Before long, feelings of awe and thanksgiving settled over me and I never questioned my participation again.

Once the process was underway none of us questioned our decisions to join the group, although we did confess to experiencing common anxieties in the days before we arrived. Several of us had prior experience with the institute and most of us were adept in communication skills and workshop modes. The younger women, with less confidence but also with less at risk, approached the project with no unique disadvantage. We all had found reason to feel misplaced at first. Without exception, we all came to see ourselves as blessed by God and privileged among women.

Why so blessed, so privileged? Certainly a gathering of women is neither an unusual nor compelling event. We each grappled with this question—a different kind of question than the one we had assembled to discuss. The answer lies, I think, in both the *ecumenical* and *institute* dimensions of our experience. With a name like the *Institute For Ecumenical and Cultural Research,* we might have anticipated what would be of value, but none of us was prepared for what we found.

All of us had been raised in established Christian churches; we brought to our table allegiance to both a common Christian faith and a variety of traditions. This diversity, rather than burdening us with politeness, procedure and church politics, actually freed us.

My own experience is an example: I was raised in a sound, faith-filled, traditional Catholic environment. An 18-year Catholic education, coupled with the gifts of faith, family and experience, cemented my religion. I enjoyed discussing academic and moral issues of church and faith, although I had limited serious religious discussion to fellow Catholics, both the disenchanted and the active. My personal faith life was never a subject.

At the institute, the rules were entirely different. Having a mandate to talk about personal spiritual matters with strangers from different traditions freed me of my usual duty to defend my own church. My sense of obligation was suspended in this environment. Where ignorance was allowed, differing views were presumed and talking about oneself was the rule.

My Catholic faith has been strengthened through this experience as well as my appreciation of other Christian traditions. This new perspective benefited us all. The greater gift, however, was being witness to a continuous expression of faith in God and trust in God's presence in each of our daily lives. The bonds of intimacy between us grew wider and more comforting the more we explored our faith experiences. And the fullness of the faith we shared as one was far greater than the sum of the articles and experiences of faith we offered individually.

If the Ecumenical Institute experience was valuable because of the group of people it assembled, it was equally so because of the setting it provided. Living at the institute for those few days each summer was personally and spiritually enriching. The environment reinforces discussion, permits peace to enter, becomes prayer. Although the important physical qualities of our living situation cannot easily be duplicated, the centerpiece of our experience—the discussion process—can be.

The process we used was an adaptation of the first-person presentation process which the Ecumenical Institute relies on in all its consultations. Our first-person narratives were not focused on a particular church issue, which is the usual way at the institute, but on whole-life stories.

Sharing life stories both requires and nurtures trust. The process asked us to be vulnerable—to express personal ideas, to acknowledge personal feelings. At the same time, the process gave us protection through honesty, freedom, love. We did trust and in return, we were given community.

There is a simplicity about a life-stories discussion process which belies its effectiveness. In our faith-sharing experience, there was also holiness. When we arrived, our aim was to surface issues concerning women's experiences with their churches. We might have encountered contentious and uncomfortable discussion: instead we were blessed with peace. Our honest, respectful explorations at the institute give hope that people of faith can come together for the good of both individual spirituality and the future of the church. The process is a blessing for the whole church.

"In fact the kingdom of God is among you" (Luke 17:21).

The institute days are challenging and wonderful, but eventually we ask ourselves some hard questions: Is this fun because we are among friends? Is it splendid because we are protecting ourselves from unpleasantness? Can we share so well because we are all smart, articulate, hand-picked for the task? Do others struggle to name God, find safety and be heard? Do others feel too big or too small for their spiritual skin, too clumsy to fly, too free to be attached? Do others notice patterns in their lives as we do—other women and also other men—and would they share their stories if the chance were theirs? Do we have something to say because we are unique, or because we aren't?

The sunlit community room at the institute, where we hold our common sessions, becomes confining. Themes and questions bounce off walls and windows like laser beams in a sci-fi film. They refuse to be still, to attach to paper. We need to test our discoveries with other groups in other places. After two summers we give ourselves a task, with extra rules and the obligation to report. This charge to research marks a departure from our initial plan. Not all of us see the need as priority. We do agree, however, that if our institute experience is to have meaning beyond that of our personal growth, we need to test our theories. The process we know is significant, but for what end would we suggest the process?

In search of answers, we agree to take our theories and our process "on the road." Using a plan we call "satellites," we will assemble groups of women in our home communities and ask them to share the stories of their faith journeys. We will look for themes and for evidence of the success or failure of the process. The gatherings will be short and less intense, of course, but modeled nevertheless on our own gatherings. We are concerned that the group experiences we offer be similar to ours and not deteriorate into group therapy sessions, theology comparisons, or other such pitfalls.

The satellite groups vary, depending on the time and determination we each give to the project. Some satellites take defined form over a number of sessions, others meet only once. Not all of us organize groups; various forms of informal surveying among friends, colleagues and church acquaintances are all that is possible for some. While informal study satisfies our curiosity, the satellite groups provide the results we need. We are not seeking validation of our experiences, for they are undeniably our own. We are seeking verification that another group would uncover, in the sharing of their experiences, themes and patterns similar to ours.

If verification was our hope as we embarked on the satellite group project, it is also our discovery. Listen to the voices from a group in Texas ...

"Each of us knows without a doubt that we are a child of God and that God watches over us and leads us to where we are needed ... we are listeners ... "

"I felt we were together because we had been called, not because of our desire ... "

"Individual stories of personal faith journeys were forthright, candid and sincere. Mutual trust in speaking and listening was apparent, resulting in instant friendship ... "

"The ecumenical nature of the group pointed out clearly that in all denominations, women have common experiences; and women in all denominations need wit, perseverance and strong faith ... "

"Sometimes we think we are the only ones struggling to make sense of how we are to fit into God's world, but there are so many others trying also."

Among the satellites is a group of eight Catholic women in Minnesota, who range in age from their 30s through their 60s and include a parish school principal, a former lay missionary and an Eastern-European immigrant. Except for the influence of doctrines on the Virgin Mary and the Communion of Saints, the themes which surfaced at that square study table are much the same as those of the mostly Protestant women in the round table in Texas: the strength of mothers, early faith, sense of protection and acceptance through God, openness to the intentions of God, willingness to live with the frailties and impediments of individual churches. Another satellite, which is sustained for many months, finds the themes of pain, oppression and reconciliation surfacing alongside those of girlhood faith and God's purposes for us in the cycles of life.

The satellites echo the thesis which we discovered in our

first days together: We may wrestle with our earthly churches, but we are secure in the God of all Christian faith.

"Pray for one another" (Jam 5:16).

A subject like "Women and the Church" is a bit like "humanities" in a liberal arts curriculum—is there anything that doesn't qualify? Well, yes, there is. In this case, it's men.

As the days of the summers' consultations unwind, our discussions around the conference room coffee table spill out into the living quarters and along the road to the abbey church and the cafeteria and the potter's studio. Prayers, narratives, reflections, anecdotes ebb and flow among us. We are audience for our thoughts, listening as incidents form patterns, patterns evolve into themes, themes clash and coincide. Broad themes of love and healing and continuity and cycles and giving up control are skewing our agenda. We are feminist enough to want to claim institutional issues such as women in the clergy and masculine interpretations of Scripture as "women's issues," but do we also dare to claim as ours those other, sweeping themes? How do the men feel about faith, or perhaps, do the men feel about faith? Do they ever feel marginalized or a part of the cycles of creation, or not in control of their spiritual journey?

Our theories have become so universal, we have unintentionally opened the door to the men. While we aren't unanimously pleased with this development, the natural next stage is to extend a satellite experience to a group of men. We conclude that the physical experience of the institute is as appropriate for a group of men as it is for us.

During the third summer of the consultation, six men join us for a portion of our session. They, as we, represent diversity of age, denomination, experience and geography.

After initial introductions among the group, the men begin their own concentrated mini-consultation, consisting of life stories, prayer and worship, writing time and common recreation. They struggle with the shortened life-stories process, but they do what was asked of them and they prepare a summary of the themes and directions which emerged from their sharing.

The men describe the burden of control: "It seems to take us a long time to learn we aren't in control." The obstacle of power: "Being accustomed to power makes it especially hard even to hear, much less to accept and appropriate, the Gospel." The apparent need to be introduced to the spiritual life through the emotional life: "In watching the pain and the healing I learned there is no need to try to figure out in advance … no need to do the calculation. It's up to God." Childhood is time past for the men, not the ever-present it is to us. Guides, often women, are usually significant in "the breakthrough" to Christian identity for the men. And they, as we, ask "Why am I here?" Their answer, as ours, is that God has a reason, usually seen only in retrospect.

While the men's reflections indicate enough similarity to our themes to confirm that we are all God's people, they also indicate that our experience of faith is not altogether the same. While this is not a scientific discovery for all of Christendom, for the women of the consultation it verifies both the distinctiveness and the commonality of the faith experiences that we are sharing.

Ultimately, the differences between our reflections and the men's do not absorb our time. Our spiritual needs as Christians—and the process by which we discover and celebrate those needs—become our focus. Nevertheless, the men's group contributes two significant ideas toward the outcome of the consultation: They offer insight into their particular masculine approaches to faith and they sharpen our conviction that the key to spiritual discovery and growth as we experienced it at the institute is not so much in masculine or feminine models as in the process of sharing and listening in the presence of God.

The prayer of one of the men participants after their gathering speaks of the expectations of all of us for the future of Christian people: "The day is not too far off, I hope, when we all—men and women—will begin to listen to the voices of women powerfully interpreting their own experience of the Christian faith."

The lone moment of sustained tension through four years of consultation occurs as we women attempt to relate the men's experience to our own. Although telling their stories has been more difficult for them, in producing their report they stun us with efficiency and order. While we are still struggling to articulate themes after many days of discussion and years of reflection, they have done so seemingly overnight. We become confused, angry, even as we are trying to be thankful. They threaten us with their product and they change the chemistry of our group when they meet with us. In the aftermath we find ourselves postured to defend or challenge them. Have these men, whom we invited to amplify our experience, taken charge of our project even as they leave? It appears so.

Recreation does re-create ... and so with a song from Gail, a peace prayer from the soul of St. Francis, a walk to dinner, we are able to realign our focus. Since we are trusting that experience is truth, we must admit that the issue of the roles of men and women in the church is obviously a real one. But for us, we once again determine to translate our experience into opportunities for other Christians. Thankful for the help given by the men's satellite group and armed with paper, pens and fresh smiles, we set about to devise a plan. By ourselves.

Lord make me an instrument of your peace.
Where there is hatred, let me sow love ...
Where there is injury, pardon ...
Where there is doubt, faith ...

"Rabbi, it is good for us to be here" (Mark 9:6).

It is a homecoming—familiar, comforting and "my how we have all grown!" both together and apart. It is our fourth summer together here. I savor the treasures each woman has given us. In each gift our God is revealed: Roberta's beautiful gestures, Gail's sweet voice, Susan's tears, Nora's grief, Helen's struggle, Terese's calm, Sandra's pain, Anne's vision, Renée's new quest, Elizabeth's continuous adventure, Barbara and her children, Joyce's loyalty, Katie's young beauty, Caroline's gentle search, Gabrielle's passion, Dianne's intensity, Marilyn's wisdom, Karen's strong faith and Grace's strong spirit.

And this summer again we tell our stories, new stories each time. We worship together and we play together. And we work: We sort our writings—on being women and Christians, on themes, on the experience here. We sort our life story notes and our satellite group notes. We shuffle, categorize, prioritize and edit. We try to write outlines. We divide into small groups and rotate from one collection of papers to another, leaving notes for the next group. We are trying to find a way to express what has happened here. We are trying to define a model or method for this blessing we have been to one another. "The process is holy" and we are trying to capture it.

But process is elusive; and holiness cannot be captured. Having looked at many groups who have lived this experience it becomes apparent that each group, like each participant, finds its beauty and its blessing in its individuality. The essence of what has happened here is not neatly structured but open-ended and flexible. It is living and growing.

Our experience does not provide a rigid model or method for others. It is, instead, the dry bones which can become the living flesh into which the Spirit, the Ruach, breathes life. We put together a few "dry bones" common to all the gatherings, ideas which became the framework for our reflections: community, security, faith, story and pluralistic ecumenism.

- Each of our groups moved surprisingly quickly from a gathering of individuals to a feeling of *community*. We have noted earlier both the tendency of women to operate relationally and the essentially communal nature of Christianity. Yet it must be noted that not all groups of women or all groups of Christians foster community, at least not in the way we found it here.

- Some of us suggested that the community was more quickly established because of the feeling of *security* or safety we found here. The group facilitators made a conscious effort at "group climate setting" directed at establishing a "safe" environment, evidenced in the ground rules and guidelines. But this climate alone does not guarantee a place safe enough to "spill the entire contents of my soul" before strangers.

- Or were we truly strangers? We each brought with us a sense of *faith*—however small or shaky—that God is always with us, that as frightening as this experience seemed initially, God's hand would be at work in our gathering. We prayed together and the importance of those times of prayer should not be underestimated. We are all Christians, united in the body of Christ. Strangers who confess to be sisters.

- And we heard *stories*—stories of biblical women and stories of the woman beside us. We told our own story and others listened, lovingly, carefully. The listening and the telling of these stories both bound us in friendship and freed us to grow as individuals.
- In hearing our stories, our differences and our sameness, we grew stronger in our own faith traditions. At the same time we grew to value and feel connected with the faith of others. We came to value our diversity, our *pluralism* and be secure enough to accept this diversity of faith stories unconditionally. We found community growing out of and into diversity. And so we return full circle to community.

Community, security, faith, story and pluralism. None of these alone is the answer or fundamental requirement for "the process." But when these "dry bones" are joined together, clothed with human flesh and touched with the breath of the Spirit, we are blessed. The process is holy.

These gifts, these blessings ...
How will we be able to offer them to the church?

The question changes as we near the end of our time together. We have a sense of what the blessings are, but now we need to discover how to offer them to others, how to pass on or communicate what has happened here. No specific product is required of our consultation, but we all feel a need to pass on what we have received. The suggestions vary from a formal report to the institute board to communication through the arts. We seem to want to begin with the "grass roots" women of the church rather than the institutional church. In plenary sessions, in the kitchen, in small group meetings, over dinner, at the beach, while visiting the pottery shop—anywhere and everywhere—we speculate:

"We could write a novel."

"What about a video of women telling life stories?"

"Or dancing? Or a dramatic presentation?"

"Maybe recordings of songs or prayers?"

"What about poetry?"

"What about all the things we have already written?"

"Why not just continue spreading the process through satellite groups? Interested members of each group could go on to begin new groups."

"We could organize retreats."

"We could write a manual about how to facilitate a group."

"Who is going to do this anyway? All of us together?"

"We could submit articles to appropriate magazines and journals."

You see how it goes. We argue the advantages and disadvantages of each one. We want to do something different. We feel limited by the written word and yet the limitations involved in communication with other media seem even more restrictive. We decide to write. Each of us chooses a topic to write on and one of us agrees to try to put them together. We seem to have chosen the book format and yet there is considerable resistance to limiting ourselves to a particular style of writing—we want it to be true and personal, poetic and dramatic.

We have decided that we want to tell a story, our story.

We have all told our individual stories. Now we each write something about our communal story. Mary and Patricia gather all the words and all the memories and our two incompatible computers and begin to write.

It takes a long time. Remember, this is a true story, a story of real women's real lives. Mary has four children, family commitments and surely a thousand committees. Patricia is a graduate student with three children and two part-time jobs. Some days we look at the photos of our group on refrigerator doors and the words and ideas fall into place. Sometimes the text is neglected for months while we must focus our energies on family, friends or work. Sometimes we gather together other members of our group for inspiration and the story is revived. Some days piles of laundry, dirty dishes or committee meetings come between us and the story. But it does not die.

Patricia and Mary sit in Mary's kitchen and shuffle printouts and rearrange outlines and ideas. And we continue to laugh and talk and cry together about the bits and pieces of our life stories. The process is holy ... wherever two or three are gathered ... Mary sits in a restaurant scribbling notes on old deposit slips. Patricia carries texts in her car to review while waiting for children at overlong, after-school events. We write our story.

Our story. It is not a collection of facts, but it is all true. The truth to be found in story must spring from real, lived experience, but it need not be attached to literal factual detail. Although much of what is here is quoted directly, not all the words are verbatim; some are colored by our faulty memories, but the content is real. The writings and the dialogue are edited, but the words belong to real women. The group agreed to provide pseudonyms and to change some details as necessary for confidentiality. Two of the women whose stories are told here are composites based primarily on women who participated in satellite groups rather than the original institute gathering, but the stories and nearly all of their words belong to real women.

This is our story and like our individual stories, we hope to find something of truth, of God, in it. If the process is holy then perhaps the story is sacramental. Helen suggests why we have found such blessing in one another's stories:

**"Our stories, our journeys,
are outward signs of God's love for us."**

9

Your Story ✤

*"Listen, my sisters—and brothers too—
and you shall hear; for we have a story to tell you."*

We began our story with the word "Listen." In our gathering we listened to one another carefully, with respect and compassion. In the individual stories we often heard echoes of our own stories and each felt, as Nora expresses, that "It is eerie and wonderful to hear others speak from and to my experience as if they have seen my soul." Woven throughout the individual stories we found patterns of the greater story of God's love for God's people.

We have told you our individual stories. But our shared story, our growth and journey together as women and as Christians, is still incomplete. Your story too is part of the greater story. This is an invitation to join us on our journey, or rather to recognize that you are already part of that journey. The time for women's voices to go unheard is past. Gather with others, remembering that where two or three are gathered in his name, Christ will be with you. It is time to tell your story.

We began the story with "Listen" and this is not the end. Women have been silent listeners and now it is time for our voices to be heard. "For everything there is a season and a time for every matter under heaven ... a time to keep silence and a time to speak" (Eccl 3:7). Now it is time to speak.

At first you may feel, as some of us did, that you have little to tell, but in the telling we discovered that everyone's story contained gifts, both for the listeners and for the teller. Marilyn comments that "Each life story carries with it the moments of struggle and tragedy, as well as seasons of celebration and self-discovery. In a sense, we all came bringing a living book of adventure, romance, dreams and drama. Each and every story blessed us."

You may be uncertain, thinking like Barbara: "I wonder what small story I have to tell you." Or you may compare your story to others and feel with Nora that "My story is a small one—not diminished or insignificant, but lacking in drama. All the intensity is there, but the script is short."

But all stories are valuable, as Nora points out: "I see myself as the muted tones in the palette while you are the bright colors around me." The muted colors are as essential to the pattern as the brilliant ones.

Karen comments that "We are mosaics of the people we've met." Every story we hear becomes part of our story. And when the colors of these stories are joined together we can see the movements and patterns in God's artistry, the dance of the Spirit in creation.

Your story, your individual spiritual journey, is part of our story of women's faith. The mosaic is incomplete without your own particular colors and patterns. We are all made in God's image and the Creator's image in its fullness is best perceived in gathering together all the unique reflections of that image in the lives of every one of God's people. Our individual stories and our journey together as women of faith are parts of the larger story of God's hand at work in the lives of God's people—women and men.

Until now the story, like our image of God, has been incomplete, partially told. If women and men are to be equals in the church as they are before God, more of the story needs to be heard. Marilyn suggests a way to reach for this equality: "One of the facts of history has been the indifference or diminution of worth or value of the female story when set next to the story of the male. Women's search for equality must begin with the claiming of the value of their story. Men's search for equality must begin with the acknowledging of that value."

Women's stories and men's stories individually and together are the story of God's people and the story of God's love for those people. We all, women and men, need to tell our stories. And we all, men and women, need to listen. But just as women's stories have only rarely been heard in the past, so too many men have not had the opportunity to tell their stories; the stories of their individual journeys have too often been lost in a stereotyped men's story. It is time to recognize and value the diversity and individuality of the stories of all God's people.

Perhaps Caroline speaks for us all when she says: "As we told our stories each year, I began to see more clearly God working in my life. I think this is something we often see only in retrospect and we can't perceive God's plan if we don't take time to reflect on the progression of our lives. The Bible is a lengthy telling of a life story—the story of the people of God—which includes many individual stories, so it only makes sense that this experience has had the effect that it did. I think that Christians everywhere, women and men, should be telling and retelling the stories of God's hand in their lives."

God's story. Your story. Our story. Tell it. Live it. Celebrate it. It is Good News.

"Speak and do not be silent, for I am with you" (Acts 18:9).

Appendix ✛

Organizing Faith-Sharing Groups
Using the Life-Stories Process

Remarks

- Groups should be co-facilitated. The presence of two leaders helps prevent "follow-the-leader" attitudes among participants and avoids the situation where one person becomes the focal point. These groups are not seminars or workshops: interaction should reflect a circular rather than pyramid model.

- Groups should consist of at least six to eight participants, for a minimum of three hours. As many as a dozen or so participants may be possible if the group is sustained. Options include a full-day retreat or a series of regularly-scheduled gatherings conducted over a length of time either predetermined or chosen by the group. The schedule should be adapted to fit the size of the group and the anticipated time frame.

- The process accommodates gatherings of single or both sexes and single- or multiple-religious denominations. The highest priorities of a gathering are the telling of the stories and the times of common prayer.
- The institute procedure required keeping notes of discussion. This may or may not be helpful in other gatherings. Notes can be a valuable resource as the process moves on, but note-taking may inhibit a sense of trust, at least in initial stages of the gatherings.
- Flexibility on the part of the co-facilitators is essential. Discussion occasionally needs to be refocused, but groups should be allowed to move by their own direction. The faith-sharing purpose of the groups should give internal discipline to the discussions.

Suggested Outline

1) Welcome and opening prayer.
   (Frequent opportunities to pray or worship together will help bond the group. They remind participants of what they have in common.)
2) Ground rules and institute guidelines.
   ("Climate setting" is important for a group to feel comfortable and to work well together. The following is a synopsis of the ground rules used at the institute, which may be used or adapted. The important thing is developing as much trust and security within the group as possible.)
   - Right to participate equally and as ourselves
   - Right to pass
   - No put-downs
   - Don't hurt others or yourself

- Help create a safe atmosphere
- Right to disagree

3) House Rules: practical facts such as availability of refreshments, rest rooms and rough outline of schedule.

4) Short introductions of all participants, using whatever scheme seems appropriate.

(The sharing of life stories is less threatening if participants already know something about everyone. Additionally, it is important that each participant hears her/his voice early in the meeting. It is an axiom of meeting dynamics that those who aren't heard from and listened to in the early going of a meeting usually remain silent for the rest of the time.)

5) Short prayer, worship or reading.

6) Life stories.

(At the institute this part of the process was allowed to absorb as much time as necessary. The time constraints of other gatherings may require a time limit for story telling. Participants should be reminded of the limit and given notice some minutes before their time is up. The focus for the stories should be repeated occasionally during the gathering. Prepare a question or a statement to help participants keep on focus. The phrase used at the institute was "Trace your spiritual journey from childhood.")

7) Break times.

(Do this as necessary between the life stories. Depending on the group size and time frame, breaks may be needed earlier. This is a time to relax, refresh, talk about other interests or sidetracks of the discussions.)

8) Other prayers, worship, songs or readings perhaps upon return from breaks and definitely after life stories.

9) Bible study, as time permits.

10) Discussion of common themes, as time permits.

(At the institute, this discussion was part of the "task" of the consultation. No such task obliges other gatherings, but the life-stories process tends to surface commonalities and links in our lives and therefore, such discussion is both inevitable and valuable. It may occur within the life-stories portion of the gathering; it may also recur at this later time.)

11) Individual writing, as time permits.

(This reflection time was used at the institute to elicit thoughts for a possible document. It is a most valuable experience for participants, even if the writings are never shared. If the group chooses, writings can be shared and discussed.)

12) Closing prayer, worship, reading or song.

Note: Groups which are sustained for a period of time may repeat the outline, with short "updates" of life stories and concentration on discussions, insights and writings.

Postscript ✥

Participants in *The Consultation on Women and the Church*, held at the Institute for Ecumenical and Cultural Research, Collegeville, Minnesota, 1985-1988:

Sue Carmichael	Claire Mathews
Molly Culligan	Mary Mathews
Vera Duncanson	Martha Nelson
Sarah Foxworth	Catherine Rolzinski
Patricia Gillespie	Elaine Ugolnik
Marina Herrera	Timothy Vann
Amy Hirshfeld	Margaret Weitzel
Linda Kulzer, O. S. B.	Beverly Zaine
Jo Anne Lyon	

In the interest of confidentiality, participants have been given pseudonyms and a few non-essential details have been changed for book preparation. Exception to the use of pseudonyms occurs when Patricia and Linda function as initiators of the project and when Patricia and Mary function as authors or editors. Patricia, Linda and Mary have been given pseudonyms when they participate as fellow members in the discussions.

The songs of Sue Carmichael, some of which appear printed in the book, are available on tape, by contacting the Episcopal Diocese of Florida, 325 Market Street, Jacksonville, FL 32202.

Additional copies of this book may be obtained
from your local bookstore
or by sending $13.95 per copy, postpaid

to:

Hope Publishing House
P.O. Box 60008
Pasadena, CA 91116

CA residents kindly add 8¼% tax
FAX orders to (818) 792-2121
VISA/MC orders to (800) 326-2671